LEGAL PROTECTION FOR THE CONSUMER

Legal Almanac Series No. 52

LEGAL PROTECTION FOR THE CONSUMER

NEW AND REVISED EDITION

by Stanley Morganstern

1973

OCEANA PUBLICATIONS, INC.

Dobbs Ferry, New York

This is the fifty-second in a series of LEGAL ALMANACS which bring you the law on various subjects in nontechnical language. These books do not take the place of your attorney's advice, but they can introduce you to your legal rights and responsibilities.

Library of Congress Cataloging in Publication Data

   Morganstern, Stanley, 1941 -
     Legal protection for the consumer.

    (Legal almanac series, no. 52)
    Appendices (p.   ): A. Wisconsin franchise
legislation. -- B. Ohio consumer legislation.
    1. Consumer protection -- Law and legislation --
United States. I. Title.
KF1610.M65   1973   343'.73'07   73-12278
ISBN 0-379-11086-5

Manufactured in the United States of America

TABLE OF CONTENTS

INTRODUCTION

"The consumer is moving forward. We cannot rest content until he is in the front row, not displacing the interest of the producer, yet gaining equal rank in representation with that interest. What is new is the concern for the total interest of the consumer, a recognition of certain basic consumer rights: The right to safety, the right to be informed, the right to choose, the right to be hear." President Johnson (1964)

These words of President Johnson have set the tenor of consumerism for the 1970's. The old adage of caveat emptor, let the buyer beware, no longer applies to consumer transactions. To the contrary, the seller is now the one who must beware, and the future will bring an even further swing of the pendulum from favoring the seller to favoring the buyer.

Both the federal government and the state and local governments have worked diligently in promoting the consumer. The number of agencies whose function is to aid the buyer is becoming endless. Legislative enactments aimed at protecting the consumer are increasing each year and cover such varied areas as home remodeling and sale of brewery products.

This almanac is an attempt to aquaint the consumer with those agencies, federal and state, which can aid him. It is an introduction to the vast area of legislation seeking to protect him and assist him in obtaining legal remedies when a seller has mistreated him.

The basis of this almanac is derived primarily from publications obtained from various state agencies which freely disseminate such information upon request. This author gratefully acknowledges the help and assistance of those agencies in preparing this almanac, and has included herein as an appendix a partial listing of agencies available to the consumer seeking help.

The typical objectives of such agencies are as follows:
"To educate and inform the public in order to to make more sophisticated consumers; To process and resolve complaints and inquiries regarding consumer transactions; To do in-depth analysis of specific industries which may need more regu-

lation." (Department of Commerce, Consumer Protection Division, State of Ohio.)

There are approximately thirty-seven states which have enacted legislation seeking to control, eliminate and punish deceptive acts and practices by sellers. Most of these states have appropriated money and manpower to enforce these acts. These agencies and the laws which they seek to enforce cannot, however, be effective unless the consumer is aware of their existance and takes advantage of the services offered.

It is interesting to note that the information supplied by these agencies is primarily directed at educating the consumer. Its message is preventive consumerism, rather than corrective. But an important function of these agencies is to correct problems that have arisen. Corrective methods include mediation, legislation and judicial action.

Areas of consumer education which are the subject of legislation include but are not limited to: buying and servicing new or used cars; borrowing, buying or building a new home; arranging or financing funerals; home appliances; insurance; real estate promotions; jewelry; home furnishing; moving and storage; utilities and transportation; guarantees; foods and drugs; false advertising; professional services; finance companies; repair services; door-to-door sales; franchises; travel agencies; magazine subscriptions; mobile homes and many others.

The President's Advisory Council on Consumer Affairs has established goals for successful consumer education:

1. A rudimentary understanding of a market economy and the consumer's position in it, particularly his responsibility to make intelligent choices,

2. Knowledge of standards of quality and an ability to translate the technical jargon often used by manufacturers and advertisers into everyday language,

3. Knowledge of sources of information about products,

4. Knowledge of existing legislation and regulatory agencies that serve consumers,

5. An alertness toward fraudulent and misleading advertising and all other fraudulent schemes,

6. General understanding of the legal rights and recourse of consumers,

7. Knowledge of certain goods and services and what features to look for when making buying decisions.

Of course this almanac cannot cover all of the problems in each of these areas, but it will present some case histories provided by the various state agencies. These histories are illustrative of typical problems and how they are solved.

The educational aspect of the various consumer protection divisions cannot be over emphasized. Many of the agencies have employed such diverse means as preparing curriculum and course material for use in schools, both on an adult and student level, radio and television spots, speakers for community and social groups, and mailings of educational material.

The scope of consumer protection activities in Michigan was described by Frank J. Kelly, Attorney General:

"It has been our endeavor to mobilize the resources of law enforcement agencies, business organizations, service clubs, labor organizations and other public and private clubs in the war against consumer frauds. We have initiated legislation, fought successful civil law suits, brought criminal actions against individuals and organizations, engaged in educational programs and taken other actions designed to make Michigan an unpleasant place for consumer fraud activities."

These activities are typical of the efforts of consumer divisions throughout the United States. To explore each of the divisions and the legislative enactments would require several volumes, but we shall present the most typical statutes and explore in some detail the ways and means by which a consumer can prevent and correct consumer frauds in many areas. These include not only direct frauds by misrepresentations of price, quality, warranties and the like, but also deceptive advertising practices, home soliciations, and all other areas where the consumer is at the mercy of the seller.

3

Chapter 1

HISTORY OF CONSUMERISM

As illustrated in the Introduction, consumerism is fast becoming a watchword of our times. Caveat emptor no longer is applicable. Public reaction to and indignation with shoddy and fraudulent consumer practices has led to the initiation of legislation and the creation of numerous consumer protection agencies.

Earliest consumer activities in the United States involved attempts at assuring quality in foods. The entire country was shocked out of its complacency by Upton Sinclair's The Jungle. This expose of the meat packing industry led to the first food and drug legislation.

In 1938 Congress enacted the Wheeler-Lea amendment to the Federal Trade Commission Act of 1914. This act expanded the area in which the Federal Trade Commission could protect consumers by eliminating the need to establish that the act complained of had limited competition, as was previously required.

Through the years the jurisdiction of other federal agencies has been expanded, and extensive federal legislation has been enacted for consumer protection. Among the later ones are Truth-in-Securities, Truth-in-Lending and Truth-in-Packaging legislation.

Extensive state legislation has been enacted contemporaneously with federal legislation. Each of the state laws seeks to eliminate "unfair or deceptive acts" or practices in many areas. These laws will be examined in detail later.

Among the federal agencies which have been established or expanded to aid the consumer are the Interstate Commerce Commission, the Utilities and Transportation Commission, the Food and Drug Administration, the Department of Social and Health Services, the Department of Agriculture, the Securities and Exchange Commission, the Federal Trade Commission, and advisory groups to the President on consumer affairs.

The judiciary, too, has and is taking an active part in consumerism. Of course, the courts must have the basic tools with which to work -- statutory enactments -- but a vast body of law is developing in the courts. An important tool which the courts have recently invoked is Section 2-302 of the Uniform Commercial

Code. That uniform piece of legislation has been adopted by all the states except Louisiana and, in general, governs most consumer transactions.

Section 2-302 permits a court to declare that a particular clause or an entire contract is unconscionable and results in oppression or unfair surprise to a consumer. There have been four very recent cases which have applied the theory of Section 2-302 and have resulted in decisions helpful to the cause of consumerism.

In American Home Improvement, Inc. v. MacIver, 201 A. 2d 886, the court refused to enforce a contract because the value of actual services rendered to a consumer was far below the contract price. Only $959 of a total price of $2,568 was representative of actual services rendered.

A referral sales program whereby color televisions were sold to consumers who would refer other customers for a commission gave rise to a second case. Upon delivery of the goods, the contracts were immediately discounted. A New York court hearing that case, captioned State by Lefkovitz v. ITM, Inc., 275 NYS 2d 303, held that the contracts were unconscionable under Section 2-302 of the Uniform Commercial Code and thereby laid to rest the doctrine of caveat emptor.

In Frosttifish Corporation v. Reynoso, 274 NYS 2d 757, the transaction was held to be unconscionable because the service charge almost equaled the price of the goods sold.

The New York court held:

> "It is normally stated that the parties are free to make whatever contracts they please so long as there is no fraud or illegality --
>
> However, it is the apparent intent of the Uniform Commercial Code to modify this general rule by giving the courts power to police explicitly against the contracts or clauses which they find to be unconscionable. The principle is one of the prevention of oppression and unfair surprise."

In Williams v. Walker-Thomas Furniture Co., 350 F. 2d 445, a District of Columbia court refused to enforce a contract which provided that goods purchased earlier from the same seller remained as security for later purchases. A default on the new debt could result in the consumer having to surrender all the goods he purchased from that seller even though some had actually been paid for in full. Such a contract is unconscionable and, hence, unenforceable.

The doctrine of <u>caveat</u> <u>emptor</u> is, therefore, slowly but surely being eliminated by operation of the courts, statutory enactments and administrative agencies. A consumer no longer knows just what he is buying or from whom he is buying. Certainly consumers lack the technical knowledge to be able to ascertain the quality of the products they buy. Without aid and assistance, the consumer in today's complicated market place would be at the mercy of the vendor.

The doctrine of <u>caveat</u> <u>emptor</u> has been traditionally applied between a lessor and a lessee. Now, however, an expanding number of states have changed the traditional rule to include what amounts to an implied warranty of habitability flowing from the lessor to the lessee.

A recent Iowa case held that a tenant is entitled to a habitable dwelling, free from latent defects and material housing code violations. These warranties are to be given either orally or in written form and can be included in the written lease of the dwelling house, condominium or apartment. A breach of the implied warranty of habitability occurs, according to the Iowa court, when any of the following factors appear:

1. The alleged defects violate building codes, ordinances, or regulations;

2. The deficiency or defect has a negative effect on safety and sanitation;

3. The defect has persisted for an unreasonable length of time;

4. The amount of rent does not justify less than habitable conditions;

5. The tenant did not voluntarily, knowingly and intelligently waive the defects;

6. The defects and deficiencies did not result from abnormal, unusual, or malicious use of the premises by the tenant.

Thus, it can be seen that caveat emptor, even in this traditional stronghold of the doctrine, is dwindling in importance. The situation of landlord-tenant is not the only area where the courts and legislatures have ventured to relegate the doctrine of caveat emptor to a minor role.

The State of Ohio has, for example, enacted a home solicitation sales act which went into effect on January 1, 1973. That law applies to all sales, whether cash or financed, where the purchase price is $35.00 or more, when the contract is signed in the buyer's home.

The law provides that the buyer has the right to cancel the contract by giving written notice to the seller, to be delivered or mailed not later than midnight of the third business day after and not including the day the contract was signed. This right of re-scission is in addition to that the buyer might have under the Federal Truth-in-Lending law. The following paragraph must appear in the contract.

Buyer's Right to Cancel

You may cancel this agreement or purchase by mailing a written notice to the Seller postmarked no later than midnight of the third business day after the date this agreement was signed. You may use this page as that notice by writing ''I hereby cancel'' at the bottom and adding your name and address. The notice must be mailed to:

_____
(name and address of seller)

The caption as shown must be centered over the statement and printed in solid capital letters of not less than twelve-point bold-face type. The remaining words of the statement must be in type at least two points larger than the type used in the contract or purchase agreement. The warning must appear conspicuously in the contract and must be adjacent to or above the buyer's signature lines.

Failure to include the above warning on the part of the vendor may result in a fine of up to $1,000.

Thus, consumerism has rapidly expanded from a concern for edible foods to a vast range of consumer-protection legis-lation and intricate procedures of state and federal agencies. The courts, too, have taken up the cause for consumerism and these trends in legislation and judicial decisions will be explored throughout the remaining chapters of this almanac.

Chapter 2

FEDERAL AND PRIVATE AGENCIES

While the majority of this almanac deals with state legislation and state consumer agencies, the consumer should not forget that the federal government, through its various agencies, has sought to protect the consumer. Most federal agencies, however, are not concerned with individual grievances but rather are concerned with areas and products which affect the consuming public in general. Such agencies include the Food and Drug Administration, the Securites and Exchange Commission, the Federal Trade Commission, the Public Health Service, the Interstate Commerce Commission, the U. S. Postal Service, the Federal Communications Commission, and the Department of Justice.

The Food and Drug Administration is concerned mainly with hazardous substances, food, drugs, cosmetics, and any other product which could be harmful, flammable or likely to cause injury, death or loss of property.

One area in which the Food and Drug Administration has taken particular interest is toys. Particularly at Christmas time, the consuming public becomes aware that manufacturers are placing on the market children's toys which in many ways can cause injuries. The Food and Drug Administration has sought to regulate the distribution of such toys and to eliminate them from the market place. The Food and Drug Administration also becomes involved in such wide and diverse areas as labeling and inspection of food and drugs in the United States, radioactivity in food and drugs, and any other activity which tends to assure the safety and effectiveness of products traveling through interstate commerce.

While the Securities and Exchange Commission may not at first blush appear to be a consumer protection agency, it certainly is with respect to protecting the consumer who invests in stocks and bonds. The function of the commission is to regulate the issuance, sale and distribution of such securities, to assure that the consuming public is not being taken advantage of in that area.

The Federal Trade Commission has become one of the most important federal agencies participating in consumer protection.

The commission has expended a great deal of time and effort in holding public hearings to hear complaints by individual consumers. Although these complaints are heard, the Federal Trade Commission, like other federal agencies, does not attempt to adjust these complaints, but rather is concerned with the public at large. The Federal Trade Commission is vested with authority to enforce a great number of federal acts pertaining to particular products and practices. One of its prime purposes is to enforce the laws relating to false advertising and other unfair and deceptive practices. It regulates pricing practices, all advertising practices, and, in some ways, anti-trust practices. This agency works very close with other federal agencies and a complaint which originates in the Post Office Department, for example, may be adjuted or prosecuted through the Federal Trade Commission. The commission has authority to conduct formal hearings, to issue cease and desist orders, and in general, to enforce the statutes with which it is concerned.

The Post Office Department is primarily concerned with the prevention and suppression of fraud through use of the mails. Like the other federal agencies, it is concerned with those practices which on a national scale have violated the rights of consumers.

Without specifically exploring the other federal agencies, the consumer should be aware that the federal government has provided machinery with which to combat unfair consumer practices and there exists a federal agency for almost any conceivable kind of practice which affects the consuming public in general.

Beyond the federal agencies, the state agencies, and the local agencies, there are numerous private or semi-private organizations which in some measure contribute to the consumer protection scheme. For example, there are better business bureaus, labor union services, legal referral services, credit unions, family service agencies, and various trade associations.

There are also several voluntary consumer organizations such as Consumers Union, the National Consumer's League, the Consumer Federation of American and the American Council on Consumer Interests. Each of these organizations plays an important part in aiding the consumer in his buying habits, his financial arrangements, and the processing of grievances which may exist. The consumer should make himself familiar with those agencies which are available to him either through his job, union affiliation, or trade association. Trade associations have for a long period of time sought to assure the quality of goods being produced and distributed by members of their particular association. These efforts have included quality testing, quality certification and correct labeling.

The efforts of the federal government have, beyong the creation and operation of the various agencies mentioned, included consumer advisory committees reporting directly to the President of the United States. In March, 1962 President John F. Kennedy created a Consumer Advisory Committee, and in 1964 President Johnson appointed a Consumer Representative to his White House Staff. Congress, in the meantime, has been examining auto insurance, automobile and appliance warranties, job safety, mine safety, door-to-door sales, and many other areas of consumer interest.

While these federal and private agencies are available to the consumer, the state agencies, state legislation and state enforcement practices provide, perhaps, the most workable and effective means of consumer protection.

Chapter 3

STATE LEGISLATION

Since there is at the present time no standard uniform state law covering the various areas of consumerism, it is necessary to examine at least a few of the individual state laws. Generally, these acts cover a wide variety of consumer problems and punish the sellers or advertisers who commit practices in violation of the laws. These acts may be called deceptive trade practices and deceptive advertising acts. Many states combine the two main areas into a single law while others have enacted separate and distinct laws on each subject.

The enforcement of the laws is generally vested in the state attorney general's office, who, with the aid of investigatory powers and the courts, prosecutes the vendors who have violated any provision of the acts. Most of the state laws, while often providing severe civil and criminal penalties, do not abrogate the consumer's right to bring a private lawsuit. Many, in fact, provide explicitly for such suits and dicatate the awarding of double or triple damages along with costs of suit and attorney fees.

While it is not possible to review thoroughly each of the states and each of the state enactments, we shall summarize the consumer legislation of many states. The reader should be aware, however, that an in-depth study of the particular statute in question should be made before seeking to apply it to his particular situation.

ALASKA

In 1970 Alaska enacted an Unfair Trade Practices and Consumer Protection Act. Under that act the following practices are unlawful:

1. To fraudulently convey or transfer goods or services by representing them to be those of another;

2. To falsely represent or designate the geographic origin of any goods or services;

11

3. To cause possible confusion as to the source, sponsorship, approval, affiliation or association with or certification of goods or services, or to actually misrepresent such approval, sponsorship, etc;

4. To represent used goods as new;

5. To misrepresent the quality of goods or services;

6. To disparage the goods and services of another by false or misleading representations;

7. To advertise goods or services with the intent not to sell them as advertised;

8. To mislead by advertising that goods are available for sale when in fact there are not enough of such goods to supply a reasonable demand;

9. To mislead as to the reasons for, existence of, or amounts of, price reductions;

10. To engage in any other conduct which would damage a buyer or competitor;

11. To employ deceptive practices, fraud, false pretense or the like in the sale or advertisement of goods and services whether or not any person has actually been mislead, deceived or damaged;

12. To fail to meet the disclosure provisions of the act as to installment sales contracts.

Although the Alaska statute appears to be most thorough in its inclusion of possible deceptive practices, other acts done by vendors, though not included in the codified law, may be subject to civil lawsuits brought under traditional common law principles. Criminal prosecutions arise from intentional and knowing violations of the statute.

Since the act includes advertising provisions, the typical exemptions are found. Owners and publishers of newspapers, and television and radio station owners and operators are excluded so long as there is no knowing participation in the unlawful act. Likewise, advertisements governed by other federal and state statutes do not fall within the application of this particular statute.

The attorney general of the state is authorized to investigate alleged violations of the act, to prosecute offenders and to obtain injunctions. The courts can return monies or property to the consumer who has been damaged by reason of the unlawful act. Written assurances of future compliance may be obtained.

The act specifically authorizes private or class actions by consumers. The courts in such actions may award the consumer his actual damages or two hundred dollars, whichever is greater. Willful violations of the act, proved in a civil suit, may result in treble damages or equitable relief if warranted.

Interestingly, the Alaska statute is unique in that it requires the plaintiffs in a class action to post a bond in the sum of five thousand dollars. In the event the plaintiffs do not prevail in the litigation, the bond may be used to cover the defendant's costs and attorney fees incurred in defending the suit. Many statutes allow the plaintiff to recover attorney fees in such suits, but do not give parity to the defendants if they are successful. This one does just that and appears to be most equitable.

A civil action may be commenced within two years from the time the consumer discovers, or reasonably should have discovered, his loss.

Another interesting provision of this statute makes manufacturers or suppliers of merchandise which is the basis for the action liable for the damages assessed to, or suffered by retailers charged under the statute. Penalties for violation of the provisions of the statute are, as in many other states, rather severe. A violation of an injunction can result in a fine up to twenty-five thousand dollars for each and every violation. Other violations of the statute may cost the offender from five to ten thousand dollars.

ARIZONA

The Division of Consumer Fraud was created in the state of Arizona in 1966. That division is aided by state legislation which makes unlawful any practice, fraud, misrepresentation or the like, employed in consumer transactions. Likewise, the omission of any material fact in the advertising of goods and services is an unlawful act under the Arizona statute.

An act or omission may be unlawful despite the fact that

13

the consumer has not actually been misled or damaged by the misrepresentation. The deceptive act or omission in and of itself is all that is necessary to constitute an unlawful act.

Any advertisement which amounts to an attempt to induce a person to enter into any obligation or acquire any title or interest in any merchandise is covered and regulated by the statute. Such advertisement may be by publication, solicitation or any writing. As in most other statutes regulating advertising, owners of newspapers, publishers, and owners and operators of television and radio stations are exempt from the Arizona statute. In addition, all advertisements subject to or in compliance with the rules and regulations of the Federal Trade Commission are exempt from the operation of this particular statute.

The attorney general of Arizona is empowered to investigate verified written complaints. He may require the charged party to file a written statement concerning the transaction complained of. He may examine, under oath, persons connected with the transaction, and may examine the merchandise, samples thereof, as well as any pertinent books and records of the seller charged with violating the state statutes governing consumer protection.

Once a violation is detected by the attorney general, he is empowered to seek and obtain an injunction. This judicial restraint on activities prohibits the vendor from continuing practices which violate the particular sections of the consumer protection act he has already violated. The courts of Arizona may restore to the injured consumer all monies or property, real or personal, which were lost as a result of the unlawful practice by the vendor. The court may go so far as to appoint a receiver whose function is to make sure the funds or property are returned to the injured consumer.

Since the prime purpose of this type of state consumer protection statute is to assure that violations once found will not recur, the attorney general is authorized to have the violater execute a written statement of future compliance. This written statement is to be filed with the court and strictly complied with by the seller who has signed such.

If any person violates the terms of an injunction or court order, he is subject to a maximum fine of ten thousand dollars. Any person who willfully and intentionally violates any provision of the Arizona statute and is convicted therefore is guilty of a criminal misdemeanor and subject to imprisionment of up to six months and a fine of up to ten thousand dollars, or both.

While the statute contains criminal or monetary civil

penalties, it does not bar a civil suit brought by the aggrieved consumer in his own name. In all actions prosecuted by the attorney general, the guilty party may be required to pay all costs of the action including a sum representing reasonable attorney's fees for the services rendered by the attorney general's office.

INDIANA

The Indiana statute deliniates those practices which are deemed to be unfair consumer practices. These are:

Sec. 3 (Deceptive Act) (a) The act of a supplier in representing, orally or in writting, as to the subject of a consumer transaction furnished by such supplier, any of the following is a deceptive act:

1. That such subject of a consumer transaction has sponsorship, approval, performance, characteristics, accessories, uses or benefits it does not have which the supplier knows or should reasonably know it does not have;

2. That such subject of a consumer transaction is of a particular standard, quality, grade, style, or model, if it is not, and if the supplier knows or should reasonably know that it is not;

3. That such subject of a consumer transaction is new or unused, if it is not, and if the supplier knows or should reasonably know that it is not;

4. That such subject of a consumer transaction will be supplied to the public in greater quantity than the supplier intends or reasonably expects;

5. That replacement or repair constituting the subject of a consumer transaction is needed, if it is not, and if the supplier knows or should reasonably know that it is not;

6. That a specific price advantage exists as to such subject of a consumer transaction, if it does not, and if the supplier knows or should reasonably know that

it does not;

7. That the supplier has a sponsorship, approval or affiliation in such consumer transaction he does not have, and which the supplier knows or should reasonably know that he does not have;

8. That such consumer transaction involves or does not involve a warranty, a disclaimer of warranties or other rights, remedies, or obligations, if the representation is false and if the supplier knows or should reasonably know that the representation is false; or

9. That the consumer will receive a rebate, discount, or other benefit as an inducement for entering into a sale or lease in return for giving the supplier the names of prospective consumers or otherwise helping the supplier to enter into other consumer transactions, if earning the benefit is contingent on a sale or lease occurring after the consumer enters into the original consumer transaction.

A deceptive act may also result from representations within a product or on its packaging. Such false representations constitute a deceptive practice not only on the part of the supplier who places the misrepresentation thereon, but also as to any other supplier who states orally or in writing that the representation is true, so long as the supplier knew or had reason to know that the representations were false.

The supplier is not, however, without a possible defense to the action. If the supplier can show by a preponderance of the evidence that the act resulted from a bona fide error, even though he maintained reasonable procedures to avoid such errors, the act will not be a deceptive one within the meaning of the act. A second defense is also available to the supplier. He may establish that the deceptive act was done in good faith, without his knowledge of its falsity, and in reliance upon the representations of the manufacturer.

Civil lawsuits are authorized under the Indiana statute and may take the form of individual or class actions. In either case the court may award actual damages and reasonable attorney fees incurred in prosecuting the action.

The attorney general of Indiana is empowered to seek injunctions against deceptive acts and in general to enforce the various provisions of the Consumer Protection Act. The Consumer Protection Division is a part of the attorney general's office and he is granted authority to investigate claims, mediate claims, and prosecute offenders. The division is also instructed to initiate and maintain an educational program to inform consumers of deceptive sales practices.

IOWA

Like many other states, Iowa has a consumer fraud act which was originally enacted in 1965 and amended in 1970. It is a combination of the advertising and unlawful business practices which many states have adopted as separate statutes.

The act provides that no person shall use any deception, fraud, false pretense, false promise, misrepresentation or concealment, oppression or omission of any material fact so that others rely upon such concealment, suppression or omission in connection with the sale or advertisement of any merchandise, whether or not such person has in fact been mislead, damaged, or deceived thereby. The employment of such practices is an unlawful practice under the act. Likewise, any person who in the advertisement for sale, lease, rent, etc. offers such goods or services at a price which includes a rebate contingent upon the procurement of prospective customers is engaging in an unlawful practice. Any contract which contains such contingent sales price rebate is null and void as to those provisions, but enforceable as to the actual sale, lease, or rental agreement.

There is a specific provision in the act as to the offering of sale or advertising of subdivided lands. Any person who is advertising or selling subdivided lands must first file certain plans, plots, diagrams of water, sewage and electric lines, etc. with the real estate commission of the state. The failure to file or the filing of mistatements constitutes and unlawful practice.

The office of the attorney general in Iowa is empowered to administer and enforce provisions of the consumer protection acts of that state. In so doing, he is conferred the power to subpoena persons, to conduct public hearings, and to provide such forms and promulgate such rules and regulations as may be necessary. Any information which is provided to the attorney general during his investigation or public hearings relating to possible unfair practices under the act cannot be admitted in a

17

criminal prosecution. If there is a subsequent criminal prosecution relating to the subjects testified to or the evidence gathered by the attorney general, the state has the burden of establishing that the information so provided was not used in any manner to further the criminal investigation or prosecution.

The 1970 amendment to the Iowa act takes that provision one step further, and provides that when a civil action is brought the attorney general has the right to require any defendant to give testimony, but no criminal prosecution based upon the transactions about which the defendant is questioned and required to give testimony shall be thereafter brought against such defendant. This, then, amounts to an immunity from criminal prosecution once a civil action is brought and the defendant is required to testify in that civil action or in the investigation of that civil action.

Once the attorney general begins his investigation and employs his subpoena power, a defendant who fails to respond to that subpoena is subject to judicial punishment. A court, based upon the attorney general's allegations of refusal to abide by this subpoena, may grant injunctive relief restraining the sale or advertisement of any merchandise by such persons. Further, the court may dissolve a corporation created under the laws of the state of Iowa or may revoke or suspend the certificate of authority of a foreign corporation doing business in that state or may grant such other relief as required under the circumstances.

The attorney general is authorized to obtain injunctions against persons who are engaging or are about to engage in an unlawful practice as established by the act. The courts further are authorized to return any monies or properties which may have been acquired by means of any practice declared unlawful by the terms of the act. To insure the return of such monies or property the court may appoint a receiver.

A receiver, once appointed, has the power to sue, collect, receive and take into his possession all the goods and chattels, rights and credits, monies and effects, lands and tenements, books, records, documents, papers, chose in an action, bills, notes and property of every description which were obtained by the defendant by any practice declared to be illegal and prohibited by the act. If the property was commingled with the properties rightfully belonging to the defendant, the receiver has the authority to sell and convey the property so as to return the rightful amount to the person who has suffered damages by reason of the unlawful practice.

Since the act contains unfair advertising provisions, the normal exclusions as to owners or publishers of newspapers, magazines or printed matter are provided. Owners and operators of radio or television stations are granted exemptions. These exemptions are, of course, based upon the fact that the owner, publisher or operator has no knowledge of the intent, design or purpose of the advertiser. Advertisements which comply with the rules and regulations of the Federal Trade Commission are, of course, exempt from application of the state act. The state of Iowa Department of Justice, Office of the Attorney General, Consumer Protection Division has published a manual known as "Consumer Protection at the State Level." It is written by Douglas R. Carlson, Assistant Attorney General, Consumer Protection Division. In that manual appears, perhaps, the best explanation of procedures under a consumer fraud act.

The first step under the typical consumer fraud act is the receipt of a complaint either by letter or telephone. The consumer protection division or the attorney general, as the case may be, will usually next contact the company or individual against whom the complaint is filed. The purpose of the initial investigation is to determine whether or not the complaint has any merit. On the one hand, the claim may be warranted but there may be insufficient evidence of fraud to proceed upon the claim. On the other hand, the claim may be groundless.

After the initial investigation has been completed, the further dispostion of the claim depends primarily upon the attitude of the potential violator. Well established, reputable companies will normally adjust the complaint as soon as it is brought to their attention. Thus, there is what may be referred to as a mediation stage. If the complainant and the violator are willing to adjust the matter, then, in most cases, the complaint will not be carried any further. If, however, the complaint cannot be mediated, the result might be a lawsuit brought in the name of the state or a civil lawsuit brought in the name of the individual consumer. Most companies are desirous of protecting their reputations and obviously want to adjust claims before the lawsuit stage.

In those states which employ criminal prosecution as deterrance to unfair practices, the complaint may result in the criminal prosecution and the levying of substantial fines.

This procedure of enforcing the state's statutes can be employed instead of, or contemporaneously with, the bringing of a private lawsuit.

KENTUCKY

The Division of Consumer Protection in the state of Kentucky was created to encompass the following activities:

1. To promote the coordination of consumer protection activities that all departments, divisions, and branches of state, county, and city government are concerned with;

2. To assist, advise, and cooperate with federal, state, and local agencies and officials to protect and promote the interest of the consumer public; to advise the governor and the legislature in all matters concerning consumer affairs;

3. To conduct investigations, research studies, and analysis of matters affecting health, safety, the human environment, the market place, and all other consumer affairs and take appropriate action; to communicate the view of the consumer to state, county, and city agencies and officials;

4. To study the operation of all laws, rules, regulations, orders, and state policies affecting consumers, and recommend to the legislature new legislation, rules, regulations, orders, and policies in the consumers' interests;

5. To organize and hold conferences on problems affecting consumers, to undertake activities to encourage business, industry, and the professions, and others offering goods or services, to maintain high standards of honesty, fair business practices, and public responsibilities in the production, promotion and sale of consumer goods and services;

6. To provide a central clearing house of information for all citizens of the commonwealth by collecting and compiling consumer complaints and inquiries and forwarding them to the proper governmental agencies if appropriate;

It shall be the further responsibility of the

division to maintain records indicating the final disposition by the agency of any matter so referred;

7. To organize, promote, and conduct consumer education programs within the commonwealth; to cooperate with and establish necessary liason with consumer organizations;

8. A. To appear before any federal, state, or local governmental branch, commission, department, rate-making or regulatory body or agency to represent and be heard on behalf of consumers' interest;

   B. To be made a real party in interest to any action in behalf of consumer interests involving a quasi-judicial or rate-making proceeding of any state or local governmental branch, commission, department, agency, or rate-making body, whenever deemed necessary and advisable in the consumers' interest by the attorney general;

9. To perform such other acts as may be incidental to the exercise of the functions, powers, and duties set forth in the Kentucky revised statutes.

These powers, duties, and functions of the division that have been set forth are representative of the powers, duties, and functions of most of the states' consumer divisions.

The unlawful practices statute of Kentucky makes it unlawful to engage in false, misleading, or deceptive acts or practices while in the conduct of any trade or business. This includes actual fraudulent misrepresentation in the sale of goods or services and in the advertisement of same. The normal exemption for owners or publishers of newspapers, and owners or operators of radio or television stations are provided for in the statute.

The attorney general in the state of Kentucky is empowered to enforce the unfair practices statute and is granted the right to seek injunctive proceedings in the state courts. The attorney general may obtain a restraining order when he establishes, to the satisfaction of the court, that a consumer is about to suffer immediate harm, loss, or injury from the acts or practices of a vendor. The vendor then has the opportunity to seek a dissolution of that restraining order by judicial process.

21

Like courts in other states, the courts in Kentucky are authorized to appoint receivers to assure that consumers will receive their monies or properties payed to a vendor as a result of the unfair practice.

Consumers are authorized to bring civil actions when they have actually suffered damages by reason of the unfair practices committed against them in any transaction which is made for a personal or family reason. The consumer may receive actual monetary damages or, in the proper cases, equitable relief. Further, the consumer may receive punitive damages as a punishment to the vendor for committing such unlawful practices. In addition, a plaintiff in such action is entitled to a reasonable amount as attorney's fees and his costs of suit. Such civil suits must be brought within two years after the actual violation of the Kentucky law, or within one year of the attorney general terminating any action with respect to that transaction, whichever is later.

The attorney general is authorized to accept written assurance of voluntary future compliance by any person, firm, corporation, or business which has committed an unfair practice or is about to commit such unfair practice. This voluntary assurance is not to be considered an admission of violation for any purpose, but simply provides to such business, the opportunity to show its good faith and to adjust the complaint made.

The attorney general of Kentucky has subpoena power and the power to fully investigate any complaint by gathering all documentary evidence needed for that investigation.

In addition to the general unfair practice statute, Kentucky has enacted a referral selling law. That act prohibits the seller or lessor from giving or offering a rebate or discount to the buyer or lessee as an inducement for sale or lease in consideration of the buyer giving to the seller the names of prospective purchasers, or otherwise aiding the seller or lessor in making a sale or lease to another person. Of course, to be an unfair practice the rebate, discount, or other value must be contingent upon an event subsequent to the time the buyer or lessee agrees to buy or lease. If a violation of this provision occurs, the agreement is unenforceable and the buyer or lessee may at his option rescind the agreement or retain the goods delivered and the benefit of any services performed without any obligation to pay for them.

Kentucky also has a typical homes solicitation sales act. Homes solicitation is defined under that act as "a sale of goods or services in which the seller or person acting for him engages in a personal solicitation of the sale at a residence of the buyer and the buyer's agreement or offer to purchase is there given to the seller or a person acting for him.'' It does not include a sale made persuant to prior negotiations between the parties at a business establishment or a fixed location where goods or services are offered or exhibited for sale.

A home solicitation may be cancelled by the buyer until midnight of the third business day after the day on which the buyer signs an agreement or offer to purchase. Cancellation occurs when notice is given, and the mailing or posting of the cancellation is sufficient. Cancellation need not be in any particular form.

In one instance, however, a buyer may not cancel a solicitation. If the buyer requests the seller to provide the services without delay because of an emergency; and the seller in good faith makes a substantial performance of the contract before the buyer gives notice of cancellation; and the goods cannot be returned in substantially the same condition as received by the buyer; a cancellation will be ineffective.

Although the buyer may cancel the transaction by any written expression of his intention to cancel, the seller is under an obligation to provide the buyer with a written statement. That statement must appear as follows: ''If this agreement was solicited in your residence and you do not want the goods or services, you may cancel this agreement by mailing a notice to the seller.''

The notice must say that the consumer does not want the goods or services and must be mailed before midnight of the third business day after the agreement is signed. The notice must be mailed to the address of seller given. Failure of the seller to give such notice to the buyer extends the buyer's time in which he may cancel. The buyer may cancel at any time until he has received such notification. Until he does receive such, his cancellation may be in any form whatsoever.

When a cancellation is made, the seller must tender back to the buyer any payments the buyer has made, along with any note or other evidence of indebtedness. If there were goods traded in, they must be tendered back by the seller to the buyer in substantially as good condition as when received. If the seller fails to return goods traded in, the buyer may elect to recover an amount equal to the trade-in allowance stated in the agreement.

The seller is not, however, without any redress for the

cancellation. He may retain as a cancellation fee 5% of the cash price not in excess of the cash down payment. If, however, the seller fails to comply with his obligations under this act he is not entitled to retain his cancellation fee. Until the seller has complied with his obligations, the buyer may retain possession of the goods delivered to him and is granted a statutory lien on the goods in his possession or under his control for any recovery of funds to which he is entitled.

The buyer is also under obligations when he exercises his right to cancel the agreement. He must within a reasonable time after the cancellation, and upon demand by the seller, tender back to the seller any goods delivered by the seller persuant to the sale. His obligation to tender, however, does not require him to move the goods from his residence. If the seller fails to demand possession of the goods within a reasonable time after the cancellation, the goods become the property of the buyer without any obligation on his part to pay for them. A reasonable time is defined in the statute as forty days. The buyer also has the duty to take reasonably good care of the goods in his possession for a reasonable time after cancellation. If the items involved in the sale are services rather than goods, the seller unfortunately is entitled to no compensation except his cancellation fee.

Kentucky has also legislated in the specific area of unsolicited goods. When unsolicited goods are delivered to a person, he has the absolute right to refuse to accept them and is not bound to return the goods. The act specifically provides that these unsolicited goods are deemed to be a gift to the recipient who is free to use them in any manner whatsoever after receipt, without any obligation for the payment thereof. Although the person receiving unsolicited goods is not prevented from returning the goods to the sender, the sender is, of course, taking a chance upon delivering unsolicited goods. Chances are he will receive no payment and not have the goods returned. The term unsolicited is not defined under the statute, but it does not include any merchandise requested by the recipient or merchandise which is addressed to or intended for another person and which the recipiant received by mistake.

An interesting part of the consumer protection package in the state of Kentucky pertains to used automobiles. Under that statute, it is unlawful for any motor vehicle dealer or moter vehicle salesman to refuse to furnish upon request of the prospective purchaser the name of the previous owner of any used car offered for sale. Violation of that statute can result in a fine

24

of not less than fifteen dollars nor more than two hundred dollars, or imprisionment of not more than thirty days, or both. Violations of other provisions of the Kentucky statutes can result in fines up to twenty-five thousand dollars, depending upon the particular violation.

MARYLAND

The Consumer Protection Division in Maryland was created in 1967. That agency reports now handling approximately two thousand requests and inquiries per week, in addition to performing its other functions of mediation, legislation, education, and investigation. Through the efforts of the division, the state legislature has enacted legislation covering a wide range of consumer problems, including unordered merchandise through the mail, a comprehensive system of meat inspection, referral selling, unsolicited credit cards, home solicitation sales (seventy-two-hour right to cancel), odometer setbacks, return of security deposits for tenants, phony games and prizes in promotions, and unit pricing.

Some of Maryland's enactments are of particular interest. The unit pricing law requires sellers to provide shoppers with the total price of goods sold in supermarkets as well as the unit price. This allows a shopper to compare effectively brands and sizes before choosing a product.

It is a criminal offense in Maryland to reset an odometer with the intent to defraud a prospective used car buyer. In the same piece of legislation, an automobile dealer may lose his license when he willfully refuses to honor a new car guarantee or warranty. The recutting or regrooving of tires below original tire standards is also prohibited by the act.

MASSACHUSETTS

Massachusetts has enacted a comprehensive system of consumer protection statutes. These acts cover the following subjects: false advertising; deceptive advertising of guarantees; deceptive pricing; general misrepresentations; referral schemes; advertising or offering to sell on an "easy credit" basis; repairs and services including warranties and service contracts; door-to-door sales and home improvement transactions; private home study, business, technological, social-skills and career schools -- correspondence and other; private

25

employment agencies and business schemes; lay-away plans; pricing and refund; return and cancellation privileges; subscription and mail orders; new-for-used, substitution of products; failure to deliver.

The attorney general of the state is authorized to investigate and prosecute persons or firms who have violated any of the business practices acts. While there is not a particular definition of unfair methods of competition and unfair or deceptive acts or practices in the conduct of trade or business, the act does specify that the courts are to be guided by the interpretations given by the Federal Trade Commission and the Federal Courts to Section 5 (a) (1) of the Federal Trade Commission Act.

The advertising provisions of the statute give the following definitions which are helpful in understanding the type of practices this and other state statutes seek to prevent.

"ADVERTISEMENT," "ADVERTISING," "ADVERTISE"

Any commercial message in any newspaper, magazine, leaflet, flyer, or catalog, on radio, television, public address system, or made in person, in direct mail literature or other printed material, or any interior or exterior sign or display, any window display, in any point of transaction literature or price tag which is delivered or made available to a customer or prospective customer in any manner whatsoever is an advertisement.

"BAIT ADVERTISING"

"Bait advertising" is an alluring but insincere offer to sell a product which the advertiser does not intend or want to sell. Its purpose is to switch consumers from buying the advertised product in order to sell something else, usually at a higher price or on a basis more advantageous to the advertiser. The primary aim of a bait advertisement is to obtain leads as to persons interested in buying a product of the type so advertised.

"BLIND ADVERTISING"

An advertisement which has the tendency to induce consumers to contact the advertiser and which fails to reveal that the primary purpose of the advertisement is the sale of goods or services, and fails to reveal the identity of the advertiser is "blind advertising."

The statute prohibits the following advertising tactics:

FALSE ADVERTISING

A. No advertisement containing an offer to sell a product shall be made when the offer is not a bona fide effort to sell the advertised product.

B. No statement or illustration shall be used in any advertisement which creates a false impression of the grade, quality, make, value, currency of model, size, color, usability or origin of the product offered, or which may otherwise misrepresent the product in such a manner that later, on disclosure of the true facts, there is a likelihood that the buyer may be switched from the advertised product to another.

1. Even though the true facts are subsequently made known to the buyer, the law is violated if the first contact or interview is secured by deception.

C. No act or practice shall be engaged in by an advertiser or seller to discourage the purchase of the advertised product as part of a bait scheme to sell another product.

For example, among acts or practices which will be considered in determining if an advertisement is a bona fide offer are:

1. The refusal to show, demonstrate, or sell the product offered in accordance with the terms of the offer.

2. The disparagement by acts or words of the advertised product or disparagement with respect to the guarantee, credit terms, availability of service, repairs or parts, or in any other respect, in connection with it.

3. The failure to have available at all outlets listed in the advertisement a sufficient quantity of the advertised product to meet reasonably anticipated demands, unless the advertisement clearly and adequately discloses that supply is limited and/or the product is available only at designated outlets.

4. The refusal to take orders for the advertised product to be delivered within a reasonable period of time.

5. The showing or demonstrating of a product which is defective, unusable, or impractical for the purpose represented or implied in the advertisement.

6. Use of a sales plan or method of compensation for salesmen, or penalizing salesmen, designed to prevent or discourage them from selling the advertised product.

27

D. No practice shall be pursued by an advertiser or seller in the event of sale of the advertised product of obtaining or attempting to obtain a rescission of the sale for the purpose of selling another product in its stead. Among acts or practices which are relevant in determining if the initial sale was in good faith, and not a stratagem to sell another product are:

1. Accepting a deposit for the advertised product, then switching the buyer to a higher-priced product;

2. Failure to make delivery of the advertised product within a reasonable time or make a refund;

3. Disparagement by acts or words of the advertised product, or disparagement with respect to the guarantee, credit terms, availability of service, repairs, or in any other respect, in connection with it;

4. The delivery of the advertised product which is defective, unusable or impractical for the purpose represented or implied in the advertisement. Sales of the advertised product do not preclude the existence of a bait-and-switch scheme if the sales are a mere incidental by-product of the fundamental plan and are intended to provide an aura of legitimacy to the over-all operation.

There are specific regulations pertaining to the advertising of guarantees. Certain disclosures must be made when a guarantee is advertised. The advertisement must contain the nature and extent of the guarantee, including what the product or part thereof is guaranteed, what characteristics or properties of the product are covered, the duration of the guarantee, what the person claiming under the guarantee must do to fulfill his obligations thereunder, and the manner in which the guarantor will perform, as well as his identity.

Special attention is paid to those guarantees which are adjusted on a pro rata basis. Full disclosure of how the adjustment is to be made must be given. The Massachusetts regulations give the following example of such a guarantee and the disclosures that must be given:

Example: During the course of a sale, "A" sells to "B" for $20.00 and with a twelve-month guarantee a battery that he regularly sells for $25.00. After six months the battery proves defective. If "A" adjusts on the basis of the price "B" paid, $20.00, "B" will only have to pay one-half of $20.00, or $10.00, for a new battery. If "A" instead adusts on the basis of the regular selling price, "B" will owe one-half of $25.00, or $12.50, for a new battery. The guarantor would be required to disclose here the following: that this was a twelve-month guarantee; that the regular selling price, rather than the actual sale price, would be used in the adjustment; that there would be an adjustment on the basis of the time that the battery was used; and, that he would not pay the adjustment amount in cash, but would make an adjustment on a new battery, if such be the case.

Other disclosures must be made depending upon the type of guarantee offered.

"Satisfaction or your money back," "ten-day free trial," or similar representations will be construed as a guarantee that the full purchase price will be refunded promptly at the option of the buyer.

If such guarantee is subject to any conditions or limitations whatsoever, they shall be disclosed.

Example: A rose bush is advertised under the representation, "Satisfaction or your money back." The guarantor requires return of the product within a year of purchase date before he will make refund. These limitations, i.e., "return" and "time" shall be clearly and conspicuously disclosed in the ad.

When a product is represented as "guaranteed for life" or as having a "lifetime guarantee," the meaning of the term "life" or "lifetime" should be explained.

A seller or manufacturer shall not advertise or represent that a product is guaranteed when he cannot or does not promptly and scrupulously fulfill his obligations under the guarantee.

The term "unconditionally guaranteed" should not be used when a guarantee is restricted in any manner other than as to time, and, when there is a time limit, it should be clearly disclosed (e.g., "unconditionally guaranteed for three years"). An "unconditional guarantee" is considered as an undertaking on the part of the guarantor either to refund the full purchase price of the product so guaranteed or to repair or replace such product should it prove defective in any respect, all at the option of the buyer.

Massachusetts has a comprehensive enactment on repairs and services including warranties and service contracts. Since many other states do not have specific statutes it is set forth herein.

A. Repairs and Services. It shall be an unfair and deceptive act or practice to:

1. Fail to provide in advance to a customer upon request a written estimate of the cost to the customer of the anticipated repairs, or the basis upon which the charge to the

29

customer will be made and the reasonably expected time to accomplish such repairs, including any charge for reassembly of any parts disassembled for inspection or any service charge to be imposed;

1. Make or charge for repairs which have not been authorized by the customer;

3. Fail to disclose, in the case of an in-home service call where the consumer has initially contacted the repairman, that a service charge will be imposed even though no repairs are effected, before the repairman goes to the consumer's home;

4. Represent that repairs are indicated to be necessary when such is not a fact;

5. Represent that repairs have been made when such is not a fact;

6. Represent that the goods being inspected or diagnosed are in a dangerous condition or that the customer's continued used of them may be harmful to him when such is not a fact;

7. Materially understate or mistate the estimated cost of repair services;

8. Fail to provide the customer with an itemized list of repairs performed and the reason for such repairs, including:

> a. A list of parts and statement of whether they are new, used, or rebuilt, and the cost thereof to the customer; and

> b. The number of hours of labor charged and the name of the mechanic performing the service; provided, however, that the requirements of (b) shall be satisfied by the statement of a flat rate price if such repairs are customarily done and billed on a flat rate price basis.

B. Warranties. It shall be an unfair and deceptive act or practice to fail to perform or fulfill any promises or obligations arising under a warranty. The utilization of a deceptive warranty is unlawful.

Language intended to limit or modify the warrantor's obligations under a warranty shall not operate to limit the warrantor's liability, notwithstanding the limiting language, if the warrantor fails to perform under the warranty; provided, however, that no language of limitation otherwise unenforceable by statute or regulation shall be enforceable. This regulation in no way limits, modifies, or supersedes any other statutory or regulatory provisions dealing with warranties.

C. Service Contracts. It shall be an unfair and deceptive trade practice to fail to disclose in writing, fully and conspicuously, in simple and readily understandable language that a service contract charge will be imposed if the consumer wishes to insure that repairs will be made to a purchased product so that it will operate properly. It shall also be an unfair and deceptive trade practice to fail to disclose in writing, fully, clearly, and conspicuously, in simple and readily understandable language, that a consumer is paying a lower price for goods or services in exchange for a waiver of his warranty rights.

General provisions of the Massachusetts statute regarding private home study, business, technological, social-skills, and career schools are as follows:

A. False Advertising. The making or causing, or permitting to be made or published, any false or deceptive statement or representation, or any statement or representation which has the tendency or capacity to mislead or deceive students, prospective students, or the public, by way of advertising or otherwise concerning private home study, business, technological, career, or social-skills schools, their activities in attempting to enroll students, or concerning the character, nature, quality, value, or scope of any course of instruction or educational service offered, its influence in obtaining employment for its students, or in any other material respect, is an unfair and deceptive trade practice.

B. False Representation as to Earnings. The making of false or deceptive statements or representations or any statement or representation which has the tendency or capacity to mislead or deceive students, prospective students, or the public regarding actual or probable earnings or opportunities in any vocation or field of activity is an unfair and deceptive trade practice.

It is unfair and deceptive practice in the sale or offering for sale of consumer services for a school or person subject to this regulation to represent or imply in advertising or otherwise that persons employed in a particular position earn a stated salary or income or "up to" the stated salary or income unless certain circumstances set forth in the statute exist.

C. Misrepresentation of Opportunity. The making of false, untrue, or deceptive statements or representations, or any statement or representation which has the tendency or capacity to mislead or deceive students, prospective students, or the public regarding any opportunities in any vocation or field of activity as a result of the completion of any given course of instruction or educational service is an unfair and deceptive trade practice.

D. False Representations as to Student Employment or a School's Connection with or Approval by the United States Government or the Commonwealth. The making of false or deceptive statements or representations or any statement or representation which has the tendency or capacity to mislead or deceive students, prospective students, or the public as to services to be rendered in connection with the securing or attempting to secure employment for students, or as to the influence or connection of any school or schools with any branch, department, or establishment of the United States government or with the Commonwealth of Massachusetts is an unfair and deceptive trade practice.

It is an unfair and deceptive practice for a school or a person subject to this regulation to advertise or represent that the school or instruction course has been approved by any government agency without clearly and conspicuously indicating the scope, nature, and terms of that approval, particularly as to how the approval applies to the quality of instruction and the truth of the statements contained in the advertisement or representation. For example, and advertisement or representation shall not state "V.A. Approved," but must state, if such is the case: "V.A. education loans may be used for tuition. V.A. does not review nor guarantee the quality of instruction, nor does it guarantee the truth of the statement in this advertisement."

E. Limited Time Offers. Representing an offer to be limited as to time or otherwise when such is not the fact, with the tendency or capacity to mislead or deceive students, prospective students, or the public is an unfair trade practice.

F. Misrepresenting Offers as "Special." Representing an offer as "special" when it is in fact the school's regular offer is an unfair and deceptive trade practice.

G. Fictitious Prices. Offering courses of instruction at prices purported to be reduced from what are in fact marked up or fictitious prices is an unfair and deceptive trade practice.

H. Money Back Agreements. It is an unfair and deceptive trade practice for any private school subject to these regulations to use, directly or indirectly, any so-called money-back guarantee, refund agreement, or other similar guarantee, agreement, or contract between school and student.

I. Misleading Scholarship Offers. Making offers of scholarships or partial scholarships in such a manner as to mislead or deceive students or prospective students into the belief that such offers are real when in fact they are not is an unfair and deceptive trade practice.

J. Misuse of the Word "Free." Representing any commodity or service as "free" when in fact such commodity or service is regularly included as part of the course of instruction or service is an unfair and deceptive trade practice.

K. Deception in Issuance of Diplomas, Degrees. It is an unfair and deceptive trade practice for any private school subject to these regulations to issue any certificate or diploma or to confer any degree which misrepresents the course of study or instruction covered or completed or the accomplishments or standing of the student receiving such certificate, diploma, or degree.

L. Misrepresenting Faculty. Making a statement or representation through advertising or otherwise that a certain individual or individuals are members of the faculty of the school or are members of its advisory board or authors of its instructional material when they are not, or when they provide no or only token services or advice, or the making of statements or representations as to the value of any former connection with the United States government or the Commonwealth of Massachusetts as an aid to securing employment which are false or misleading is an unfair and deceptive trade practice.

M. Misrepresentation as to Personal Instruction. The representation through advertising or otherwise that students are given personal instruction by the head of the institution or a department head thereof who provides no or only token instruction is an unfair and deceptive trade practice.

N. Deceptive "Help Wanted" Advertising. The use of "help wanted" or other employment columns in a newspaper or other publication to get in touch with prospective students in such a manner as to lead such prospective students into the belief that a job is offered is an unfair and deceptive trade practice.

O. Blind Advertising. The use of "blind" advertisements or sales literature to attract prospective students when such advertisements or literature fail to set forth that courses of instruction or other educational services are being offered is an unfair and deceptive trade practice.

P. Deceptive Language in General. The use of language in any form which has the tendency or capacity to mislead or deceive students, prospective students, or the public is an unfair and deceptive trade practice.

Q. Unqualified Students. Inducing the enrollment or retention of a student for any course of instruction or training for a job or position for which the school knows or has reason to know the student is unfit by reason of educational or permanent physical disqualification or other material disqualification is an unfair and deceptive trade practice.

Massachusetts has also seen fit to protect consumers from unduly harsh collection techniques. While federal legislation prohibits what amounts to extortionate credit collection techniques, very few states have gone as far as Massachusetts in limiting extra-judicial collection policies.

That act provides: "No one who is a creditor, or an assignee of a creditor, of a natural person present or residing in Massachusetts who has incurred a debt primarily for personal, family, or household purposes shall collect or attempt to collect such debt in an unfair, deceptive, or unreasonable manner."

Under the statute, it is illegal for creditors to use unfair or deceptive practices to collect money owed to them by debtors.

A creditor may not tell or threaten to tell the debtor's relatives, employer, or other close associates about the debt in an attempt to encourage payment. However, a creditor may notify a credit bureau about the debt. But he must tell the creditor he is going to do so. Creditors also must notify debtors if they intend to hire an agent or attorney to collect the debt.

It is illegal for creditors to send debtors collection notices in envelopes that indicate or imply that a debt is owed.

It is illegal for a creditor to contact a debtor directly if the debtor has asked the creditor to deal with his attorney.

The creditor may not send the debtor forged or "legal-looking" documents to imply that court or legal action has been taken against the debtor.

It is illegal for a creditor to contact the debtor in a way that might harrass or embarrass the debtor.

The creditor MAY NOT telephone the debtor at unreasonable hours, telephone the debtor repeatedly and frequently, threaten to use violence if the debtor does not pay, use offensive language in talking to the debtor, nor threaten to take any action against the debtor that is not usually taken in his type of business.

MISSOURI

The state of Missouri has enacted legislation which it entitles "Merchandising Practices." This piece of legislation generally follows the pattern of other state legislation dealing with unfair practices to the consumer. The term merchandise as used in the caption of the statute and within its various provisions includes any objects, wares, goods, commodities, intangibles, real estate, or services.

Under the terms of the act it is unlawful to use or employ any deception, fraud, false pretense, false promise, misrepresentation or concealment, suppression or omission, in connection with the sale or advertisement of any merchandise.

The administration of the statutory provisions are vested in the attorney general of the state who may investigate and prosecute alleged violators of the statute. Injunctions may be obtained and any person who violates the terms of an injunction faces a penalty of up to five thousand dollars for each violation. Prosecution by the attorney general does not prohibit any civil action by an individual consumer.

The Missouri statute also encompasses a section on unsolicited merchandise. When unsolicited merchandise is delivered to a consumer he may either refuse to accept delivery of it or, if he wishes, he may treat the merchandise as a gift and thereafter use or dispose of it in any way he wishes. In so doing, he incurs no obligation to the seller.

NEW HAMPSHIRE

In 1970, New Hampshire enacted a statute designated as "Regulation of Business Practices for Consumer Protection." This particular act combines general unlawful or deceptive trade practices with false and misleading advertising. It generally contains the standard provisions describing the acts which shall constitute deceptive or unlawful trade practices. These include the procedures of vendors which would, in all likelihood, cause confusion or misunderstanding among consumers as to the characteristics, ingredients, benefits, or quantities of merchandise; and also confusion as to the identity of the goods, their sponsorship, approval, or certification. Likewise, the desparaging of the goods and services of another by false or misleading representations constitutes a deceptive practice under the New Hampshire statute. One who advertises the sale of goods or services, but does not intend to supply reasonably expectable public demand, or who makes false or misleading statements of fact concerning the reasons for existence of or amounts of price reductions is in violation of the act.

One who claims an exemption under the act has the burden of establishing that exemption. Publishers, broadcasters, and the like, who disseminate information without knowledge of its deceptive character, are exempt from the act as are transactions which are covered by Federal Trade Commission regulations. The attorney general is vested with authority to enforce the provisions of the act, and may establish such rules and regulations as are necessary or desirable for the proper administration of the act. The attorney general may seek temporary or permanent restraining orders against those persons who violate or are likely to violate provisions of the act. Prior to taking any specific action, the attorney general must give the alleged violator ten days notice, thus providing him with the opportunity to amicably adjust the situation. Violation of the deceptive trade practices act is a misdemeanor and a violater thereof may be fined up to one thousand dollars. If an injunction is issued and then violated, the fine can be as high as ten thousand dollars for each violation.

As in all consumer protection statutes, the person or division authorized to enforce the statute is granted investigatory rights including the power to subpoena books, records, and the like, along with examining persons who can shed some light upon the alleged violation. Failure to abide by requests of the attorney general in securing this information can result in fines up to five thousand dollars. If it is found that a particular violator, American or foreign, is one who habitually violates the injunctions granted under the auspices of the statute, the attorney general may petition the court for dissolution, suspension, or forfeiture of that corporation's right to do business in the state.

A civil suit for restitution of all goods or services lost by the consumer is authorized by the statute and the court in hearing such a case may award, along with restitution of goods or monies, all legal costs and expenses incurred by the plaintiff in the prosecution of the lawsuit. It is interesting to note that the act specifically provides that in those cases where the cause of action is based upon confusion of identity of goods and/or manufacturer, sponsor, or the like, the plaintiff is required to prove only that such confusion or misunderstanding is likely and not that it actually transpired.

NEW MEXICO

New Mexico has divided its consumer legislation into three basic areas: unfair trade practices, false advertising, and the land subdivision act.

An unfair or deceptive trade practice is defined in the

statute as: "any false or misleading oral or written statement, visual description or other representation of any kind, knowingly made in connection with the sale, lease, rental, or loan of goods or services, in the extension of credit for a collection of debts by any person in the regular course of trade or commerce which may tend to or does deceive or mislead any person, and includes: . . ." The inclusions under that definition are the standard deceptive trade practices: confusion of the identity of goods; confusion as to the affiliation; representing used goods to be new; falsely misrepresenting the quality or grade of the goods; disparaging the goods and services of another by false or misleading representations; failure to intend to supply a reasonable demand for the goods; and the like.

Unique in the New Mexico statute is a provision that packaging goods for sale without authorization in a container that bears a trademark or trade name identified with goods formerly packaged in the container is an unfair trade practice. This, of course, would be a violation of federal statutes on trademark regulation.

The act distinguishes between a "deceptive trade practice" and an "unconcionable trade practice." The latter means any act or practice in the sale, lease, rental, or loan, or in connection with the offering for sale, lease, rental, or loan, of any goods or services, or in the extension of credit, or in the collection of debts, which to a person's detriment: (1) takes advantage of the lack of knowledge, ability, experience, or capacity of a person to a grossly unfair degree; or (2) results in a gross disparity between the value received by the person and the price paid.

The civil fine for violating either the deceptive trade practices act or the unconscionable trade practice act may be as high as five thousand dollars per violation.

The act also covers chain referral sales and strictly prohibits the use of that technique whereby the buyer is induced to purchase merchandise or services upon the promise that he provide the seller with prospective buyers. In return, he will receive a reduction of the price of the goods he purchased by means of a cash rebate, commission, or credit toward the balance due.

It is also a specific violation of the act to willfully misrepresent the age or condition of any motor vehicle. Such misrepresentations include, but are not limited to, resetting the odometer, regrooving the tires, or chassis repair without previously informing the purchaser of the vehicle that such repairs were done. Anyone who violates that section of the act is deemed guilty of a misdemeanor. The seller of any motor vehicle must, at the time of the sale, provide the following information to the buyer: a description of the vehicle; a statement that to the best of the seller's knowledge there has been no alteration or chassis repair due to a previous wreck; a statement as to the mileage on the vehicle at the time of the sale; a statement that to the best of the seller's knowledge the odometer has not been altered.

As under other statutes, the attorney general is granted authority to seek restraining orders, make settlements of alleged violations and investigate all claims through the use of subpoena power and the like. The act specifically provides for private remedies and in certain incidents the court may award attorney's fees to the prevailing party.

The false advertising act in New Mexico is substantially the same as in other states. It prohibits false advertising which in any way is misleading. This includes not only representations made by statements, but also failure to reveal facts in the advertisement.

Like other states in which sale of land for development purposes is a booming business, the state of New Mexico has enacted a land subdivision act to control such business and to prevent frauds upon consumers. Basically the statute is one of disclosure, and the seller of subdivided land must make written disclosure to the purchaser of the following items:

1. All restrictions or reservations of record which subject the subdivided land to any unusual conditions affecting its use or occupancy;

2. The fact that any street or road facilities have not been accepted for maintenance by governmental agencies when such is the case;

3. Availability of all public utilities in a subdivision, including water, electricity, gas, and telephone facilities;

4. If water is available only from subterranean sources, the average depth of such water within the subdivision;

5. Complete price in financing terms or rental;

6. The existence of blanket encumbances, if there are any, on such subdivision unless such blanketing encumbances provide for a proper release or subordination to such lot or a parcel.

Advertising standards are also provided in the act and willful violation of the advertising standards resulting in misrepresentations can be punished by conviction of a felony, including imprisonment for not more than five years or by a fine of not more than $100,000 or both.

OHIO

Ohio has created a Department of Commerce Consumer Protection Division whose stated purposes are to:

Educate and inform the public in order to make more sophisticated consumers;

Process and resolve complaints and inquiries regarding consumer transactions; and

Do in-depth analysis of specific industries which may need more regulation.

The program of consumer protection is administered through the state attorney general's office and the teeth of the program are the consumer protection statutes enacted in 1972. Home solicitation sales have been examined previously and the Ohio act is in general comparable to other states' legislation which has been analyzed in detail. The cooling-off period is provided for all sales of thirty-five dollars or more consummated in the consumer's home.

The Consumer Sales Practices Act permits the attorney general to bring an action to obtain a declaratory judgment that an act or practice violates the provisions of the act. Restraining orders may be obtained against violators, and a supplier who violates such an order is subject to a penalty of up to five thousand dollars for each day of violation.

Class actions may be brought on behalf of consumers who have been damaged by acts of suppliers in violation of the statute, and consumers may recover, depending upon the type of suit brought, actual damages, property or funds paid, rescission of the transaction, injunction, or other appropriate relief.

Although the Ohio statute speaks of "suppliers" as those persons subject to the provisions of the act, that term includes sellers, lessors, assignors, franchisors, and any other person engaged in the business of affecting or soliciting consumer transactions, whether or not he deals directly with the consumer.

Deceptive acts and practices as well as unconscionable acts or practices are unlawful whether they occur before, during, or after the actual transaction. A clear, concise explanation of the types of practices prohibited was published by the Department in a fact sheet, available for public reading.

Deceptive transactions include charging an extra fee (above the estimated repair price) to take an appliance out of the home for repair unless the consumer is informed of this extra charge before the appliance is removed to the repair shop; advertising an item on sale but failing to have an adequate supply of items to meet the demand; using "bait and switch" techniques in a sales transaction; misrepresenting an item pictorially in an advertisement; delivering a product that is defective and then refusing to correct the defect or adjust the price; failing to make delivery of a purchased item within a reasonable length of time; making claims about a product which are untrue -- for example, to claim an automobile has had only one owner when it has had many. It is also deceptive to turn back the odometer on a car.

Unconscionable acts or practices are differentiated from deceptive practices by the additional feature of knowledge on the part of the supplier or a particular consumer's inability to protect himself because of physical or mental infirmities, ignorance, illiteracy, or inability to understand the language of the agreement. The fact sheet published by the division gives these examples of unconscionable acts or practices:

> Charging an exorbitant price for services or merchandise available at a much lower price;
>
> Persuading consumers to enter into transactions from which the consumer receives no substantial benefit;
>
> Making misleading statements which are likely to be of detriment to the consumer;
>
> Encouraging the consumer to enter into a contract

40

for which the supplier knows the consumer will be unable to meet payments.

PENNSYLVANIA

In 1968, Pennsylvania created a Bureau of Consumer Protection. Its duties and functions include investigatory powers of commercial and trade practices, fraud, misrepresentation, and deception in the sale, servicing, and financing of consumer goods and products. The primary piece of legislation in Pennsylvania upon which the bureau relies is the Unfair Trade Practices and Consumer Protection Law.

Unfair methods of competition and unfair or deceptive acts or practices are defined in the act. Unfair methods of competition and unfair or deceptive acts or practices mean any one or more of the following:

Passing off goods or services as those of another;

Causing likelihood of confusion or of misunderstanding as to the source, sponsorship, approval, or certification of goods or services;

Causing likelihood of confusion or of misunderstanding as to affiliation, connection, or association with, or certification by, another;

Using deceptive representations or designations of geographic origin in connection with goods or services;

Representing that goods or services have sponsorship, approval, characteristics, ingredients, uses, benefits, or quantities that they do not have, or that a person has a sponsorship, approval, status, affiliation, or connection that he does not have;

Representing that goods are original or new if they are deteriorated, altered, reconditioned, reclaimed, used, or secondhand;

Representing that goods or services are of a particular standard, quality, or grade, or that goods are of a particular style or model if they are of another;

Disparaging the goods, services, or business of another by false or misleading representation of fact;

Advertising goods or services with intent not to sell them as advertised;

Advertising goods or services with intent not to supply reasonably expectable public demand, unless the advertisement discloses a limitation of quantity;

Making false or misleading statements of fact concerning the reasons for, existence of, or amounts of price reductions;

Promising or offering to pay, credit, or allow to any buyer any compensation or regard for the procurement of a contract of purchase with others.

Home solicitation sales of twenty-five dollars or more may be cancelled in Pennsylvania by written notice within two full business days following the sale. The consumer must return the goods purchased and in return the seller must return all payments or other considerations given for the sale.

Civil penalties for violation of an injunctive order may result in a fine of up to five thousand dollars for each violation, and, in addition, the attorney general may seek the dissolution, suspension, or forfeiture of the corporate franchise of any corporation found to have violated the terms of an injunction.

RHODE ISLAND

Rhode Island, like several other states, has enacted a Home Solicitation Sales Act. Under that particular statute, both the seller and buyer have certain obligations. These are as follows:

Seller's obligations on cancellation.

(a) Except as provided in this section, within twenty (20) days after a solicitation sale has been cancelled the seller shall tender to the buyer any payments made by the buyer and any note or other evidence of indebtedness.

(b) If the down payment includes goods trades in, the goods shall be tendered in substantially as good condition as when received. If the seller fails to tender the goods as provided by this section, the buyer may elect to recover an amount equal to the trade-in-allowance stated in the agreement.

(c) The seller may retain as a cancellation fee five per cent (5%) of the cash price, five dollars ($5.00) or the amount of the cash down payment, whichever is least. If the seller fails to comply with an obligation imposed by this section, or if the buyer avoids the sale on any grounds independent of his right to cancel under this chapter, the seller is not entitled to retain a cancellation fee.

(d) Until the seller has complied with the obligations imposed by this section, the buyer may retain possession of goods delivered to him by the seller and has a lien on the goods for any recovery to which he is entitled.

Buyer's obligations on cancellation.
(a) Except as otherwise provided, within twenty (20) days after a home solicitation sale has been cancelled, the buyer, upon demand, shall tender to the seller any goods delivered by the seller pursuant to the sale, but he is not obligated to tender at any place other than his own address. If the seller fails without interference from the buyer to take possession of such goods within twenty (20) days after cancellation the goods shall become the property of the buyer without obligation to pay for them.

(b) The buyer shall take reasonable care of the goods in his possession both prior to cancellation and during the twenty (20) day period following. During the twenty (20) day period after cancellation, except for the buyer's duty of care, the goods are at the seller's risk.

(c) If the seller has performed any services pursuant to a home solicitation sale prior to its cancellation, the seller is entitled to no compensation except the cancellation fee provided in this chapter. If the seller's services result in the alteration of property of the buyer, the seller shall restore the property to substantially as good condition as it was in at the time the services were rendered.

If a buyer is to cancel the transaction, he must do so not later than midnight three (3) days following his signing the agreement, excluding Sunday and any holiday on which regular mail deliveries are not made. The notice must be sent by registered or certified mail.

A home solicitation sale can only be effective to bind a consumer if the seller provides him with notice of the consumer's right to cancel. The statute sets forth the precise written notice which must be given to the consumer.

Notice to Buyer: (1) Do not sign this agreement if any of the spaces intended for the agreed terms to the extent of then available information are left blank. (2) You are entitled to a copy of this agreement at the time you sign it. (3) You may at any time pay off the full unpaid balance due under this agreement, and in so doing you may be entitled to receive a partial rebate of the finance and insurance charges. (4) The seller has no right to enter unlawfully your premises or commit any breach of the peace to repossess goods purchased under this agreement. (5) You may cancel this agreement if it has not been signed at the main office or a branch office of the seller, provided you notify the seller at his main office or branch office shown in the agreement by registered or certified mail, which shall be posted not later than midnight of the third calendar day after the day on which the buyer signs the agreement, excluding Sunday and any holiday on which regular mail deliveries are not made.

In addition to the home solicitation act, Rhode Island has also enacted a Deceptive Trade Practices Act, and it generally follows the pattern of other state statutes which we have already examined. That statute does, however, provide for private and class actions and those provisions, as illustrative of other states so providing are set forth herein.

Private and class actions.

(a) Any person who purchases or leases goods or services primarily for personal, family, or household

44

purposes and thereby suffers any ascertainable loss of money or property, real or personal, as a result of the use or employment by another person of a method, act, or practice declared unlawful by this act may bring an action under rules of civil procedure in the superior court of the county in which the seller or lessor resides, is found, has his principal place of business, or is doing business, or in the superior court of such county as is otherwise provided by law, to recover actual damages or two hundred dollars ($200), whichever is greater. The court may, in its discretion, award punitive damages and may provide such equitable relief as it deems necessary or proper.

(b) Persons entitled to bring an action under subsection (a) of this section may, if the unlawful method, act, or practice has caused similar injury to numerous other persons similarly situated and if they adequately represent such similarly situated persons, bring an action on behalf of themselves and other similarly injured and situated persons to recover damages as provided for in subsection (a) of this section. In any action brought under this section, the court may in its discretion order, in addition to damages, injunctive or other equitable relief.

(c) Upon commencement of any action brought under subsection (a) of this section the clerk of court shall mail a copy of the complaint or other initial pleading to the attorney general and, upon entry of any judgment or decree in the action, shall mail a copy of such judgment or decree to the attorney general.

(d) In any action brought by a person under this section, the court may award in addition to the relief provided in this section, reasonable attorney's fees and costs.

(e) Any permanent injunction, judgment, or order of the court shall be prima facie evidence in an action brought under this act that the respondent used or employed a method, act, or practice declared unlawful by this act.

TEXAS

As we have seen, some states have seen fit to enumerate specifically the practices which are deemed to be unfair while others simply leave that determination to judicial or administrative interpretation. Texas has enumerated unfair practices in its statute. These practices are:

Passing off goods or services as those of another;

Causing confusion or misunderstanding as to the source, sponsorship, approval, or certification of goods or services;

Causing confusion or misunderstandings as to affiliation, connection, or association with, or certification by another;

Using deceptive representations or designations of geographic origin in connection with goods or services;

Representing that goods or services have sponsorship, approval, characteristics, ingredients, uses, benefits, or quantities that they do not have or that a person has a sponsorship, approval, status, affiliation, or connection that he does not have;

Representing that goods are original or new if they are deteriorated, altered, reconditioned, reclaimed, used, or second hand;

Representing that goods or services are of a particular standard, quality, or grade, or that goods are of a particular style or model, if they are of another;

Disparaging the goods, services, or business of another by false or misleading representations of fact;

Advertising goods or services with intent not to sell them as advertised;

Advertising goods or services with intent not to supply reasonably expectable public demand, unless the advertisement discloses a limitation of quantity;

Making false or misleading statements of fact concerning the reasons for, existence of, or amounts of price reductions;

Engaging in any act or practice which is deceptive to the consumer;

Advertising of a liquidation sale, auction sale, or other sale fraudulently representing that the person is going out of business;

Conduction or sponsoring in connection with the sale of, or offer to sell, goods, merchandise, or anything of value, any contest, sweepstakes, puzzle, or game of chance by which a person may, as determined by drawing, guessing, matching, or chance, receive gifts, prizes, discounts, coupons, certificates, or gratuities if such contest, sweepstakes, puzzle, or game, or the promotion of such contest, sweepstakes, puzzle, or game:

Misrepresents by any means or in any form the participant's chances of winning any such gifts, prizes, discounts, coupons, certificates, or gratuities; or

Fails to disclose to participants in such contest, sweepstakes, puzzle, or game on a permanent poster in case such contest or game is conducted by a retail outlet, or, in case such contest or game is not conducted in a retail outlet, on any card game piece, entry blank, or any paraphernalia required for participation in such contest or game the following:

The geographical area or number of outlets in which the contest or game is proposed to be conducted; an accurate description of each type of gift, prize, discount, coupon, certificate, or gratuities to be made available;

The minimum number of and minimum amount of cash gifts, prizes, discounts, and gratuities to be made available and the minimum number of each other type of gift, prize, discount, coupon, certificate, or gratuity to be made available.

The Texas act contains the normal exemptions for transactions covered by federal agencies, the owners and operators of advertising media, and publishers. Transactions in the insurance business which are covered by other legislation are also exempt. Restraining orders are authorized under the act when it appears that a vendor has engaged in or is about to engage in an unlawful act. The consumer credit commissioner, through the Division of Consumer Protection, is vested with the authority to conduct investigations, require the filing of reports, examine alleged violators, examine the merchandise or samples thereof, and generally do anything necessary and proper to conduct a thorough investigation of any alleged violation of the consumer protection act.

Attempts to thwart the commissioner in his investigation procedure may result in a jail sentence or a fine of not more than five thousand dollars or both. Other penalties under the act may result in fines up to ten thousand dollars.

VERMONT

Vermont has enacted a consumer fraud statute which is enforced by the consumer protection bureau of the state attorney general's office. That legislation is to complement the operation of federal statutes and decisions governing methods of unfair competition and practices. The over-all purpose, is, of course, to protect the public and to encourage fair and honest competition. The act was first put into effect in 1967. The act, beyond specifying unlawful practices, encourages activities to educate consumers in the ways of the market place and to generally promote consumer welfare.

The advertising provisions of the Vermont laws do not apply to owners and publishers of newspapers and magazines and further exempt owners of television and radio stations. These exemptions are included for the obvious reason that such persons cannot absolutely control or, in many cases, be aware of the nature of the advertisements appearing in their publications or on their airways. However, the exemptions to such owners, publishers, or operators are not absolute. They must not have knowledge of the fraudulent intent of the advertiser.

This particular statute allows the attorney general to initiate rules and regulations pertaining to unfair methods of competition and deceptive trade practices. The act provides a right of rescission where the consumer has not received a substantial portion of the goods or services he contracted for, so long as he exercises that right of rescission by delivering or mailing the notice of rescission to the seller's principal place of business on the business day following the day of the transaction. When a rescission is so made, the seller must return to the consumer any monies paid for the goods or services and any and all documents evidencing the consumer's indebtedness to the seller which documents were executed as part of the transaction being rescinded.

The rescission provisions apply to all types of goods and services including, but not limited to, automobiles, mobile homes (when used for personal use), family or household chattels, and also goods used in the area of home improvements, and construction of real property whether or not these are to become fixtures.

Services are likewise included in the rescission provisions, including all types of labor and other services to be used for personal, family, or household reasons.

An important provision of the Vermont statute is the elimination of the holder-in-due-course concept. The holder of a promissory note or other instrument of indebtedness of the consumer takes that note or instrument subject to all the defenses, real or personal, that the consumer would have against the seller in an action on a simple contract, so long as the note or other instrument of indebtedness has been delivered in connection with the contract of purchase signed by the consumer.

An agreement or a cognovit provision of a note is void and of no force and effect against any party. Likewise an assignment of wages is void.

The act specifically sets forth certain practices which if found to exist are taken to be evidence of fraud. Included in such group of prima facie fraudulent acts are the failure to accept the terms and conditions as advertised. These activities create a rebuttable presumption of intent on the part of the seller to defraud the consumer.

Like most of the other state statutes, the Vermont statute authorizes the attorney general to investigate a complaint and bring an action in the name of the state seeking a temporary or permanent injunction. The state courts are authorized to issue such injunctions and are authorized to revoke a certificate of authority of a corporation which has been found to have violated the deceptive trade practices act. The attorney general may obtain an assurance of discontinuance, that is, a written statement of the seller that he will not, in the future, violate the provisions of the act.

The attorney general in making investigations has the power

to subpoena relevant books, records, and memoranda of the sale which shed some light on the alleged violation.

Once a seller has been notified of the alleged violation and attempts to conceal, hide, or destroy any documentation pertaining to the sale, he is subject to a fine of five thousand dollars. The failure to comply with the request of the attorney general for the production of relevant documents can result in the seller being found in contempt of court. Once an injunction has been granted, the failure to abide by such injunction may result in a penalty of not more than ten thousand dollars for each violation.

Civil actions brought by aggrieved consumers are not prohibited by the act. The act provides that the consumer may recover the consideration he has paid, plus a penalty of not more than one thousand dollars.

Vermont, like many other states, has specific enactments enumerating specific unfair trade practices. One such act pertains to chain distributor schemes. Under that act it is an unfair trade practice to promote chain distributorships with solicitations of investments from the public. It is an unfair practice when the scheme serves to promote an imprudent and uneconomical investment. The reason for such legislation is that many individuals do not possess commercial expertise, and are lured by the attractiveness of unrealistic profits without considering actual market conditions and the saleability of their goods or services.

A chain distributorship scheme is a sales device whereby a person, upon a condition that he makes an investment, obtains the right to solicit, or recruit for profit or economic gain additional persons who are granted licenses or rights to perpetuate the chain. The fact that the number of persons who participate is limited or the eligibility for participants is conditioned does not change the identity of the scheme as a chain distribution scheme. It is a violation of the act to promote, offer, or encourage participation in a chain distributor scheme.

Vermont also has a seller's warranty obligation statute. It is a specific violation of that act when a seller gives warranties and then fails to honor them. Express or oral warranties made to induce the consumer to purchase the goods or services must be honored. This does not mean, however, that there may not be situations where the seller would not have to honor warranties. There may be extraordinary circumstances or facts which would make the honoring of the warranty unequitable under the situation.

In Wisconsin, the Department of Agriculture is the controlling body behind the consumer protection efforts of that state.

State legislation generally prohibits unfair methods of competition and unfair trade practices. Guidelines of what unfair competition and unfair trade practices consist of are to be determined by the department through public hearings. The administrative body is then authorized to issue orders enjoining unfair practices and unfair competition.

Like other state statutes, the Wisconsin statute authorizes the bringing of civil suits and the awarding of double damages, costs of suit, and attorney fees.

Willful violations of the unfair competition or trade practices provisions of the statutes or administrative rulings may result in fines from twenty-five hundred to five thousand dollars. Suits may be brought in the name of the state and civil penalties varying from one hundred to ten thousand dollars may result, especially where there has been a violation of an injunction.

An administrative regulation makes it an unfair practice to require a buyer to sign a judgment note for the contract price of certain home remodeling when that note is signed contemporaneously with the contract of purchase. In such a case the department has ruled the contract to be void as a matter of law.

Wisconsin has a separate fraudulent advertising law. Deceptive advertising practices are enumerated and in substance are as follows:

> To fail to state the price of goods and/or services or any other conditions imposed upon receipt of the property or services advertised;

> To advertise sales of items so as to lead the buyer to believe that the goods are offered by a private individual rather than a business firm;

> To advertise for donations by any means or sell merchandise when a part of the price to be donated to an organization, unless the following disclosures are made: the minimum amount to be donated stated in dollars; the minimum percentage of the net income to be donated; the minimum percentage of the gross income to be donated.

Other filing requirements are specified in the donation sale situation.

The advertising act requires the posting of certain information by any person, firm, corporation, etc. engaged in the businesses of furs, wearing apparel, furniture, pianos, phonographs, other musical instruments, motor vehicles, stocks, or generally any form of property, real or personal, or the furnishings of any kind of service or investment. These persons must post a sign in a conspicuous place outside the place of business and in any salesroom. The name of the association of business and the actual owner must be disclosed.

The advertising of the sale of motor fuel is specifically regulated by Wisconsin statute, and over-all exemptions are provided to the owners, operators, and publishers of newspapers, magazines, and television and radio stations.

Under the statute it is a deceptive practice to misrepresent the nature of any business. One may not use the terms manufacturer, factory, mill, importer, etc., unless the business is in fact of that nature. Further, it is a deceptive practice to misrepresent the nature of prices being offered. One may not advertise that the prices are wholesale or manufacturer's prices unless the prices truly are.

The Department of Agriculture is authorized to enforce and prosecute violations of the various statutes concerning unfair business practices. Civil actions may still, however, be brought by private consumers. These actions may result in double damages, costs of suit, and attorney fees. There is a three-year statute of limitations in the bringing of such suits.

Since the Department of Agriculture must enforce the various state statutes, it has been given investigatory powers, including the right to subpoena relevant documents, and the power to obtain written statements of future compliance from those who have previously violated the acts.

Violation of the deceptive advertising provisions can bring criminal penalties of up to two hundred dollars, six months in jail, or both. Violation of injunctive orders carry fines from one hundred to ten thousand dollars.

Home solicitation sales is another area of specific legislation in Wisconsin. A home solicitation sale is defined as the selling, leasing, or offering of sale where the sale, lease, or offer is personally solicited or consummated at the residence, place of business, or employment of the buyer or at a seller's transient quarters. Transient quarters include hotel and motel rooms as well as other temporary locations.

Personal solicitation includes telephone calls, person-to-person confrontations, and mailings other than the general advertising catalogues or requests to buy at a regular business location.

Home solicitations have traditionally resulted in representations to the buyer of a unique nature. Basically, the buyer is told that he has been specially selected for an introductory offer or that the seller really doesn't want to sell anything but rather is conducting a survey, or running a test of his product. The warranties made and the sales pitches are imaginative and effective. Recognizing these sales tactics, the Wisconsin legislature has made the following misrepresentations in home solicitations sales unlawful:

> "This is a special offer only being made to a few selected people."

> "We are conducting a survey, test, or research project." (When the real objective is a sale.)

> "This is a special sales promotion offered for a limited time to a limited number of people."

> "We are giving a gift or offering a second product at a nominal charge if you buy our product at the normal price." (This may be a legal procedure if the gift or special offer is not contingent on buying the first product. The second product may be discounted, but the consumer must be made aware of the unit price of each product.)

> "We are offering this product at a special reduced price." (Again, this may be a legal sales promotion so long as there have been substantial sales of the product at the higher price.)

> "We will provide service for a longer period of time than we are obligated to under the terms of our written contract."

> "We will reduce the price of this product if you will allow us to use your name or written statement as an

endorsement for our product or service.''

It is also a violation of the home solicitation act if misrepresentations are made as to the identity of the seller, the amount of available savings, the length of the sales presentation, the delivery or performance date, the nature of the documents to be executed, and the guarantees or warranties extended.

Interestingly, it is a violation of the act if the seller does not promptly leave the buyer's premises when requested to do so.

OTHER WISCONSIN STATUTES

Among the other areas of specific legislation in Wisconsin is regulation of trade practices in the sale or offering for sale of any wholesale cut or food service plan. Likewise, practices in the building and home improvement business are regulated. Unfair trade practices in that area include model home lure, misrepresentation of the product, bait selling, misrepresentation of the capabilities of the product, the identity of the seller, price and financing, guarantees, date of completion, and maintenance requirements. Competitors may not be disparaged unfairly, and certain disclosures must be made in the contract of sale such as insurance, maintenance, description of product, terms and conditions of financing, warranties and guarantees.

The holder-in-due-course concept is eliminated in home improvement contracts. Every assignee of a home improvement contract takes that contract subject to all claims and defenses of the buyer or his successors in interest arising out of the contract. Thus, an assigne is subject to claims arising out of defects in the material or workmanship which would not affect him if he were a holder in due course under the traditional concept thereof.

A promissory note may not be used in a home improvement transaction unless the following language appears: ''This is a home improvement instrument and is non-negotiable.''

Thus, every holder of the note takes subject to all other claims and defenses of the maker or obligator.

Wisconsin has also legislated in the areas of mobile home parks, chain distributor schemes, referral selling plans, and deceptive offers of employment.

Deceptive offers of employment usually include those in which the employee is required to make a monetary investment to obtain the employment. If such is the case, any ad promoting the employment must reveal that an investment is necessary. False advertising as to the nature of the employment, amount of earnings, commissions, or other compensation to be earned is prohibited.

Like most other states that have regulated the referral selling plans, Wisconsin prohibits sellers or lessors from giving compensation under such plans, unless the compensation is given or paid prior to the sale.

OTHER STATES

Examination of the states detailed herein gives one a good idea of the type of state legislation that now exists for the consumer's protection. It cannot be urged too strongly that a consumer's particular state statutes should be examined as there are, for all the similarities, many important differences. Most importantly is the type of available remedy. Most states provide only for actions brought in the name of the state by the attorney general while a few have expanded the traditional common law in the area to include class actions under the state statute. This is of extreme importance in that a specific act by a seller may not be violative of common law principles governing consumer transactions but indeed violative of the state statute.

In addition to the states already examined, New York, South Dakota, North Carolina, Washington, and Michigan have provided this writer with materials explaining their consumer protection activities.

Michigan's activities in the consumer legislation area include the regulation of lots, parcels, units, or interests in bonds within real estate subdivisions; the regulation of advertising; regulation of the rate of interest that can be charged; regulation of home solicitation sales; regulation of home improvement installment contracts; regulation of retail installment sales; and many other areas of inspection and regulation.

North Carolina has taken particular interest in land development promotions, especially in the area of vacation and retirement land. The state has an unfair and deceptive trade practices act with a very clear and consice statement of objectives which, in reality, states the objectives of all such statutes.

> The purpose of this section is to declare, and to provide civil legal means to maintain, ethical standards of dealings between persons engaged in business, and between persons engaged in business and

the consuming public within this State, to the end
that good faith and fair dealings between buyers and
sellers at all levels of commerce be had in
this State.

In addition to the General Deceptive Trade Practices Act,
South Dakota has legislated in the areas of unsolicitated merchandise, direct solicitation, credit contracts, advertising, and
multilevel distribution plans. The latter refers to referral selling
programs or chain sales.

Endless chain sales are absolutely prohibited and are defined as:

Any scheme or plan for the disposal or distribution
of property or services whereby a participant pays a
valuable consideration for the chance to receive compensation for introducing one or more additional persons into participation in the scheme or plan or for the
chance to receive compensation when the person intro-
duced by the participant introduces a new participant.

Washington has instructed, by publication, its consuming
public that there are a great variety of public and private agencies
which can be of assistance in solving consumer problems. These
agencies include professional associations, state departments,
better business bureaus, federal agencies, and associations of
manufacturers and retailers.

While federal agencies and state agencies have been examined in some detail, better business bureaus have not been.
Washington reports that there are approximately 140 such bureaus
located in major market centers throughout the United States,
Canada, and other countries. These bureaus have three basic
goals:

1. To help maintain a free enterprise market environ-
    ment in which business can operate profitably, by
    persuading the business community to control mis-
    representation and deception in advertising and
    selling;

2. To help maintain a consumer climate favorable to
    industrial and commercial growth and vitality, by
    demonstrating to the public the willingness and
    ability of the business community, to remove the

causes of justifiable criticism of advertising and selling;

3. To help safeguard a community's buying power, by directing it into legitimate channels of business through various public information and education services.

Obviously, these goals are compatible with the objectives of consumer agencies and consumer legislation. While the bureaus lack judicial authority to prosecute grievances, their practical powers of persuasion towards reputable business may be sufficient to adjust a problem.

Legislation in Washington has produced a consumer protection law which permits the Consumer Protection Division of the attorney general's office to process consumer complaints either by means of adjustment and satisfaction or, if necessary, by litigation.

Specific areas of consumer protection activities in Washington have included employment agencies, door-to-door selling, installment contracts, and the like.

The plight of the consumer has been recognized by most of the states and accordingly they have enacted wide sweeping legislation not only to prohibit deceptive and unconscionable practices but also to provide effective means of adjusting problems, punishing violators, and redressing grievances. More importantly, however, the states through their various agencies have recognized the need to educate the consuming public.

Chapter 4

FRANCHISING

The franchise system, having experienced a tremendous growth in a relatively short period of time, is now the subject of close scrutiny, both legislative and judicial. Basic to all franchise relationships is the temendous disparity of bargaining position which exists between the franchisor and the consumer who seeks to become a franchisee.

The right of the franchisor to terminate or fail to renew a contract for no apparent reason is but one example of the perils under which a franchisee operates. Should a franchisor have unrestricted freedom to decline renewal of the franchise? One authority in the field states:

> "While the actual term of a franchise can be set for any period, ultimately the time will arrive for renewal of the franchise. A few agreements give the franchisee an exclusive option to renew. More frequently renewal is either dependent on the agreement of both parties or in the sole discretion of the franchisor. Whatever the original term of the franchise, any franchisee who has survived all other hazards will have built up some equity in the business. That equity will be in jeopardy if the franchisor has unrestricted freedom to decline renewal of the franchise." (Harold Brown, Franchising: Trap for the Trusting, Little Brown and Co., 1970, p. 26.)

Recent years have seen the growth of a body of law concerning franchise agreements. To date, there are several states which are considering fair franchising act, and there is federal legislation regulating certain aspects of automobile dealer franchise agreements with manufacturers. 15 U.S.C.A. 1221 et seq. The Dealer's Day in Court Act, as it is called, was the culmination of numerous judicial decisions respecting the rights and obligations of automobile dealers and their manufacturers. While there is federal legislation being considered with regard to the remaining franchise arrangements (Fairness in Franchising Act, S. 1967), there is currently no federal legislation to govern the operation of franchise agreements outside of the automobile industry.

Basically, the Dealer's Day in Court Act imposes a "good faith" limitation on each and every franchise agreement entered into between a manufacturer and an automotive dealer. While the Dealer's Day in Court Act does not govern other franchise problems, some of the rationale which went into the creation of the act, and the cases which were decided in the automotive industry prior to the enactment of that act are helpful in understanding franchise problems.

Once the courts decided that a franchise agreement was a valid contract, Buggs v. Ford Motor Company, 113 F. 2d 618 (1940), the majority of decisions which followed thereafter found the courts refusing to impose limitation of good faith on the power of the manufacturer to terminate the relationship. Bushwick-Decatur Motors, Inc. v. Ford Motor Company, 116 F. 2d 675 (1940); Martin v. Ford Motor Company, 93 F. Supp. 920 (1950).

Once, however, the courts began to recognize the disparity of bargaining position existing between the manufacturers and the dealers, they began in certain instances to impose that limitation of good faith. Patterson-Pope Motor Company v. Ford Motor Company, 16 S. E. 2d 877 (1941); Kane v. Chrysler Corporation, 80 F. Supp. 360 (1948).

In the Patterson-Pope case, the plaintiff-dealer was induced to make a large investment in physical plant and equipment, only to have the Ford Motor Company cancel the franchise eleven months after its inception. The court held that the dealer had the right to believe and to act on the assumption that the contract was being offered by the manufacturer in good faith and that the parties contemplated extended performance which would result in the mutual profit of both.

When a franchise agreement terminates, whether it be a refusal to renew, or a termination of a relationship existing without a written contract, the end result is a refusal by the franchisor to deal further with the franchisee. Termination and/or the failure to renew the franchise agreement are forms of a "refusual to deal." Simpson v. Union Oil Company, 377 U.S. 13 (1964).

When this refusal to deal is the result of a lack of good faith, or an unlawful purpose, the end result to the dealer is a forfeiture of his time and efforts and the expenditures that he has incurred while developing and promoting the manufacturer's products. The result, then, in these cases, is unconscionable and the fact that the contract provides for termination does not negate the drastic results on the dealer terminated.

> "Nor is it any answer to contend, as a freedom of contract theory exponent might, that where the parties have freely allocated the risks, the terminated party should live with the bargain he has made and not be the beneficiary of special judicial relief. Such medieval notions of justice or fairness are no longer justifiable, even if the enterprisers have equal bargaining power and ability.
>
> At least some consideration ought to be given to the relative burdens imposed on each of the parties by enforcing or refusing to enforce the termination provision at that time." (Ernest Gellhorn, "Limitations on Contract Termination Rights -- Franchise Cancellations," Duke Law Journal, vol. 1967, no. 3.)

As early as 1931, the courts began to impose the good faith provision on termination options, and to discount the freedom of contract theory. J. R. Watkins Co. v. Rich, et al., 235 N.W. 845 (1931). In cases not involving automobile dealers decided after the Dealer's Day in Court Act had been passed, the courts began applying good faith determination provisions of franchises existing between manufacturers and dealers other than automotive. Gaines W. Harrison & Son, Inc. v. J. I. Case Company, 180 Fed. Supp. 243 (1960).

The question then arises as to what is meant by good faith. Good faith as defined by federal legislation means:

> "the duty of each party to any franchise, and all officers, employees, or agents thereof to act in a fair and equitable manner toward each other so as to guarantee the one party freedom from coertion, intimidation, or threats of coertion or intimidation from the other party; provided, That recommendation, endorsement, expostion, persuasion, urging or argument shall not be deemed to constitute a lack of good faith." 15 U.S. C.A. Section 1221 (e).

A good number of the automotive cases have arisen under alleged arbitrary application of minimum sales requirements. For example, Madsen v. Chrysler Corp., 261 F. Supp. 488 (1966). In areas other than automobile dealers, the courts have held that a refusal to deal would be illegal if done for the purpose of pursuing a monopoly, Eastman Co. v. Southern Photo Co., 273 U.S. 359 (1927); if done as a result of a conspiracy between the franchisor and franchisees, United States v. General Motors Corp., et al. 384 U.S. 127 (1966); if done for the purpose of illegally promoting territorial or customer allocation arrangements, United States v. Arnold, Schwinn & Co., 388 U.S. 350 (1967); White Motor Co. v. United States, 372 U.S. 253 (1963).

The court in U.S. v. Arnold, Schwinn & Co., supra, cited Susser v. Carvel Corp, 206 F. Supp. 636, 640.

> The franchise method of operation has the advantage, from the standpoint of our American system of competitive economy, of enabling numerous groups of individuals with small capital to become entrepreneurs -- If our economy had not developed that system of operation, these individuals would have turned out to have been merely employees. The franchise system creates a class of independent businessmen, it provides the public with an opportunity to get a uniform product at numerous points of sale from small independent contractors, rather than from employees of a vast chain.

The court further said:

> Indiscriminate invalidation of franchising arrangements would eliminate their creative contributions to competition and force suppliers to abandon franchising and integrate forward to the detriment of small business.

The end result of franchise terminations may be a reduction in competition. As such the motive, the intent, and the purpose behind a franchisor's refusal to deal with the franchisee is unlawful, is not in good faith, and cannot be sustained.

In reviewing the "rule of reason" of the Sherman Act, the court in White Motor Company v. United States, supra, cited Chicago Board of Trade v. United States, 246 U.S. 231, 238.

> "Every agreement concerning trade, every regulation of trade, restrains. To bind, to restrain, is of their very essence. The true test of legality is whether the restraint imposed is such as merely regulate and perhaps thereby promotes competition or whether it is such as may suppress or even destroy competition."

The failure to renew alone may be actionable under the current trend of the law.

The Fairness in Franchising Act, presented to the United States Senate, states that it shall be a violation of that act for any franchisor to terminate, cancel, or fail to renew a franchise except for good cause. Good cause for failing to renew is:

> (a) "failure by the franchisee to substantially comply with those requirements imposed upon by the franchise which requirements are both essential and reasonable, or

> (b) "use of bad faith by the franchisee in carrying out the terms of the franchise."

This act, then, shifts the burden of proof from the franchisee of showing bad faith by the franchisor, to the franchisor who now must show good faith in refusing to continue the relationship.

Realistic state legislation, Massachusets Legislature (H.2279) continued the trend. Section f. thereof provides:

> f. "Anything to the contrary notwithstanding, it shall be unlawful for the franchisor or subfranchisor to fail to renew a franchise on terms then equally available to all franchisees, to terminate a franchise, or to restrict the transfer of a franchise, unless the franchisee received fair and reasonable compensation for the value of the franchise including its good-will and his contribution to the particular franchise either as a going business (unless the business shall have been terminated without the substantial fault of the franchisor or subfranchisor) or at liquidation value (in the absence of such substantial fault), due weight to be given to such franchise fees as the franchisee may have paid for the franchise. In any case, the consent of the franchisor shall not be unreasonably withheld."

The comment to that section is quite enlightening.

> "COMMENT. These restrictions on the right of renewal, termination, and transfer are designed to assure to the franchisee the value of his equity and goodwill in his business. In substance, franchisors are required to make good on their universal promise that the franchisee is purchasing and developing a "business of your own."

Delaware recently enacted legislation closely resembling the Massachusetts act and it is conceivable that the majority of states will adopt such realistic legislation in the near future.

Uniform legislation has been presented to the American Trade Association Managers which legislation would insure fair and equitable treatment of franchisees as sought by this particular plaintiff in this particular case.

Since the judiciary for the most part has not had the appropriate legislation to rely on in granting franchisees relief from improper treatment by their franchisors, several unique theories have been established upon which the needed relief could be granted.

The theories of fraud, antitrust violations, and even security regulation have been invoked by various state courts and the National Labor Relations Board in protecting franchisees.

Behind each one of these, perhaps, tenuous arguments is the effort of the courts to do justice and protect the equity the franchisee has built up, the time and effort he had devoted and reasonably compensate him for his misplaced trust and confidence reposed in the franchisor.

Although courts have traditionally refused to issue a decree enforcing a contractual relationship upon two parties where it is incumbent upon the parties to devote their best efforts in distributing a product, <u>Bach</u> v. <u>Friedan Calculating Machine Company</u>, 155 F. 2d 361 (1946), there have been several cases in which the court has disregarded that theory and imposed mandatory injunctions on the defendant.

> "We note that the Sixth Circuit, in a case involving a somewhat similar franchise agreement, denied an injunction against interference with the franchise because the Court thought it would be too difficult to enforce, <u>Bach</u> v. <u>Frieden Calculating Machine Company</u>. Any difficulty of enforcement here does not impress us. All the defendant need do is to refrain from acting in bad faith, as it has presumably so refrained during most -- if not all -- of the 29 years this franchise has existed." <u>Bateman</u> v. <u>Ford Motor Company</u>, 302 F. 2d 63, 67 (1962).

Similar injunctions were granted <u>Madsen</u> v. <u>Chrysler Corporation</u>, <u>supra</u>, and <u>Swartz</u> v. <u>Chrysler Corporation</u>, 297 F. Supp. 834 (1969).

In <u>Hoffman Candy and Ice Cream Co.</u> v. <u>Dept. of Liquor of the State of Ohio, et al.</u>, 154 Ohio St. 357 (1930), Justice Malthias wrote an astute opinion in dissenting with the majority who refused to grant a mandatory injunction requiring the parties to deal together in the future.

> "At common law a principal may discharge his agent even though there is a contract that such agency should continue for a definite period of time. In cases where resulting damages might have been collected by an action at law, specific performance is denied, but in a situation such as presented in this case, equitable relief should be awarded.

> "This is not a question of mere personal service. Plaintiff, at considerable expense, remodeled its store and devoted a portion of its space and the services of its employees to the performance of the duties prescribed by the terms of the contract entered into with the Dept. of Liquor Control. The carrying out of the decree of specific performance in this case does not represent any of the difficulties which lead courts in the cases cited in the majority of opinion to refuse relief."

In many of the cases decided under the Dealer's Day in Court Act, the courts have granted preliminary injunctions and there seems to be no difficulty in the parties continuing their relationship while these cases pend for a number of years.

There are numerous areas of franchising which may involve violation of federal statutes, primarily of the antitrust nature. While all of these cannot be examined, it is important to mention two of these as they most directly affect a consumer who is seeking to enter into a franchise relationship.

The first of these areas is the promise of a franchisor that the franchisee will be granted an exclusive territory in which to operate. Territory exclusivity has been taken to be a per se violation of the antitrust laws. That is, the mere granting of an exclusive territory alone is proof that the relationship is one that is in restraint of trade. While a franchisor may agree that he will not compete with his franchisee within a certain geographical area, he cannot prohibit other franchisees from so competing. In an effort to grant the franchise some degree of exclusivity, the franchisor may lawfully agree that he will not appoint another franchisee in the same area, but he cannot assure the franchisee that there will be no competition from other franchisees who are headquartered in a close geographic area.

The second area which the consumer should watch in entering into a franchise agreement is a requirement that he purchase all products, supplies, and the like from the franchisor. These provisions, known as tying agreements, are illegal under the antitrust laws. The leading case in this area is Siegal et al. v. Chicken Delight, Inc., 448 F. 2d 43 (1971).

The United States Court of Appeals, Ninth Circuit, in hearing and determining that case held that the sale of a franchise license with attendant rights to operate a business in the prescribed manner and to benefit from the good will of the trade name does not require a forced sale by the franchisor of some or all of component articles.

The court gave this synopsis of the case. Where a trademark of licensor of several hundred franchisees operating home delivery and pick-up food stores was distinctive and possessed good will and public acceptance unique to it and not enjoyed by other fast food chains, the tying product, the license to use the trademark, possessed sufficient market power to bring within the Sherman Act the franchisees', claim for treble damages for injuries allegedly resulting from the franchisor's standard form franchise agreements requiring the franchisees to purchase essential cooking equipment, dry-mix food items, and trademark-bearing packaging exclusively from the franchisor as a condition to obtaining the trademark license. While the franchisor has some control over the quality and standards of the particular products a franchisor can use, he cannot effectively require the franchisee to purchase the products from him. This, of course, takes some of the very big profits out of the franchising arrangement, and is another step in the long chain of consumer protection.

Without going into any further detail, the consumer who is thinking about entering into a franchise relationship should be aware of the following areas of the agreement which may be in violation of antitrust legislation:

1. Price Control, including minimum and maximum prices;

2. Territorial exclusivity;

3. Restricting the class of customers to whom the franchisee may sell;

4. Restrictions as to the franchisee's source of supplies;

5. Restrictions as to competing merchandise, non-competing merchandise, and even nonrelated merchandise;

6. Inventory controls;

7. Requirements as to physical layout;

8. Requirements as to uniforms;

9. Prescription as to days and hours of business;

10. Restrictive covenant to to compete;

11. Unreasonable provisions as to length of contract and restrictions on sale or transfer;

12. Overbearing provisions as to termination or refusal to renew.
(Harold Brown, Franchising: Trap for the Trusting, p. 65)

FRANCHISE CHECK LIST

1. Be sure to investigate before investing any money or signing any written agreements. Discuss with a lawyer and other franchisees who have been operating in the same general area for at least one year.

2. Carefully examine records and accounts, checking out all operational costs.

3. Check the reliability of the firm, the length of time in business, its accomplishments, the kind of people managing and working for it, and the long range plan of action.

4. Make certain that the product is practical (not a fad or seasonal item) -- priced competitively, packaged attractively, and has wide appeal.

5. See that the sales territory is well defined, has good sales potential and growth possibilities, is an area whose residents have an income which can afford the item being sold,

and carefully survey the competition.

6.   The contract should: (a) cover all aspects of the agreement, spelling out in writing all verbal promises made, (b) indicate whether the franchise can be renewed, transferred, or terminated, (c) provide for a specific return merchandise credit policy, (d) indicate if there is a franchise fee -- what it is, (e) how much of an annual sales quota must be met, (f) if the franchisee can have other business interests, (g) if there is a fixed payment each year, etc.

7.   Make sure that training assistance, manuals, sales aides, purchasing guides, and advertising assistance are provided.

Chapter 5

INTELLIGENT BUYING

Many of the states which responded to the inquiry this writer made supplied informational pamphlets listing various areas in which consumers could protect themselves in buying and financing purchases. The following is a list, some with explanation, of the most prevalent areas of consumer pitfalls.

Don't buy in haste.

Don't be high-pressured by a slick salesman.

Don't be fooled by "golden opportunity," "once in a lifetime" bargains.

Don't pay a door-to-door salesman before checking his credentials and identification.

Don't permit a household appliance, radio, or TV set to be taken from your home for repairs without first getting a written estimate of probable repair cost.

Don't pay for a neighbor's package unless requested to do so.

Don't deal with fly-by-night merchants.

Don't be bargain-blind.

Don't accept or rely on oral promises.

Don't make unrealistic financial commitments.

Don't allow a door-to-door salesman to leave merchandise with you on approval.

Don't accept an incomplete bill for your merchandise.

The State of California instructs its consumers to listen for these words of warning:

You have won a free . . . .

I am not a salesman.

Only a few people are getting this special deal.

This is your last chance -- I will not be in the neighborhood again.

This low-priced advertised special is not for you, you want this expensive one.

Not only do you get these books, but you also get . . . . . .

It will only cost you the price of one package of cigarettes a day.

This is a great item, it is guaranteed for life.

I am in a contest -- one more order and I will win.

These statements should be an immediate warning to the consumer that the transaction may not be all that it is supposed to be. Upon hearing them or similar promises or representations the consumer's red light of caution should begin to flash.

Ohio has published and distributes a "Consumer Survival Manual." That manual gives the consumer of average intelligence a plan of operation in making any purchases. The consumer is instructed to read and understand all papers before signing them. He is told to buy only from reputable businessmen and to be skeptical of many advertising claims. He is advised to take his time in making any purchase and to investigate not only the product, but also the seller. A seller's reputation may be checked through the better business bureau, chamber of commerce, or the consumer fraud and crimes section of the state's attorney general's office.

Areas of prime concern to the Ohio manual are the "bait and switch" selling tactics, the sympathy approach to selling, home improvement and repair frauds, chain merchandising schemes, warranties and guarrantees, door-to-door salesmen, free gifts for buying, phony health products, money making at home ideas, and referral sales frauds.

Ohio has reported that its citizens are taken for more than $300,000,000 each year through inferior products, overpricing, exhorbitantly high interest rates, unneeded products or services, and fraudulent practices. The amount is staggering to the imagination when considered in the light of fifty-two states.

New York, too, spends considerable time and money in trying to educate its consumers in buying techniques. In response to this writer's inquiry of New York, several very complete lists of wise buying procedures were supplied. The following are those procedures recommended in the particular areas specified and reprinted with permission of the New York State's attorney general's office.

HOME IMPROVEMENTS

1. Get estimates from several contractors in writing.

2. Check the reliability of the contractor you want to use with local merchants and others for whom he has done work.

3. Check with local authorities regarding licensing of home

contractors, and if mandatory in your area, ask to see his license before signing a contract.

4. Have your contract dated and in writing, carefully spelling out a description of the work to be done, and including both starting and completion dates.

5. Be wary of the salesman or contractor who asks you to pay in advance, or to pay cash, instead of in the usual manner by check or money order on completion, or in installments as the contract specifies.

6. Do not sign a completion certificate unless the work is completed to your satisfaction.

7. Be certain that the contractor will clean up when the job is finished.

8. If there is a guarantee, be sure that is spells out details clearly, including the period for which the guarantee will be in effect.

9. Check with local authorities regarding a law permitting you to cancel a contract by notifying the contractor, under certain conditions.

10. Make certain that the contract includes in writing all promises made by the salesman.

11. If you need to borrow money to pay for the work, check first with your bank or other reputable financing agencies before you contract for work to be done.

12. Discuss the contract with your attorney before signing.

GUARANTEE

1. Always put it in writing -- accept no verbal promises.

2. How will the guarantee be kept? -- (Will repairs be made on damaged parts, will broken parts be replaced, will refunds be made for ineffective parts, is labor for repairs included?).

3. Who is making the guarantee -- the seller or the manufacturer? (Make sure you return the manufacturer's guarantee card -- if one is included).

4. The person making the guarantee is responsible for the true description of the product.

5. Lifetime guarantee must clarify -- whose lifetime -- product's or owner's?

6. 50% savings guarantees -- must make provisions for what will happen if this amount is not saved, and, if there are time limits involved, just what they are.

7. Satisfaction or money back guarantees -- are expected to promptly return the full purchase price -- unless stated otherwise in the guarantee.

8. Unconditionally guaranteed products -- which prove to be defective in any way, are expected to be replaced, repaired, or full purchase price refunded, and, in addition, must clearly state the time limit involved.

9. "Guaranteed" -- products will be regarded to be the same as unconditionally guaranteed, fulfilling the same conditions as well.

10. Pro rata guarantees -- must be clearly described, and based on a conspicuously placed price, since these vary according to product depreciation.

CONSUMER BUYING RIGHTS

1. No advertiser or seller can engage in the practice of discouraging the purchaser of the advertised product as part of a bait or scheme to sell another product. It is illegal in New York State under the General Business Law, Section 396.

2. Deal only with honest dealers who provide both the opportunity to buy the advertised merchandise and salesmen whose representations for the products are the same as those made in the advertisements.

3. Deal with the store which has a large stock of the advertised article.

4. Be aware that although the reputable merchant may show the customer other goods of the same kind at a higher price, he does not deliverately resist selling the advertised article, nor does he place unnecessary and untrue obstacles to deter the customer from purchasing the item.

GOOD HEALTH

1. Avoid "door bell" doctors, doctors promising quick answers and cures, and those making medical and biological diagnosis through the mails.

2. Avoid health lecturers whose "pitches" are made in small hotel rooms, admission free, with the end result being a product for sale.

3. Make sure your doctor has academic training in his field, his degree from a reputable institution, is listed in high standard professional directories, and belongs to well qualified medical organizations.

4. Do not place reliance upon medical testimonials or case histories used in advertising to promote "miraculous cures."

5. Do not purchase "quick cure" remedies, they may be dangerous to health and life when used with or without supervision. They are often worthless for the purposes for which they are intended, and they can be detrimental to actual conditions for which they are offered, sometimes even causing irreparable damage.

6. Above all, see a competent and reputable doctor when worried about your health, particularly in cases involving persistent and recurring disorders.

BUYING A USED CAR

1. Carefully inspect the car's interior and exterior -- look for signs of wear and age in:

a. broken seats, torn upholstery and pedal pads;
b. broken or ill-fitting doors and windows;
c. poorly operating brake pedal;
d. oily "scum" in radiator area;
e. rust and dampness under floor mats;
f. repainted areas along body sides.

2. Take your car for a road test -- listen for: squeaks, knocks, rattles, and unusual noises.
Look for: smooth start; tight, even steering; quick engine pickup; cool radiator (no overheating); etc.

3. Take the car to a competent and reputable mechanic for a thorough checkup.

4. Be wary of low mileage on an older car. (A good mechanic can tell if the mileage has been set back -- a practice illegal in New York State.)

5. Understand the purchase contract, thoroughly. Don't sign one with blank spaces, make sure you have a copy, and question anything you don't understand.

6. Be certain that all verbal promises are put in writing.

7. If you buy on credit, make certain you know the full purchase price of the car -- and what the interest will be.

8. Be sure, when you answer an advertisement, you see the car which was advertised -- don't be switched to a newer, fancier, higher-priced model.

9. Above all, buy from locally established or well-recommended dealers who have earned the fine reputation that they enjoy.

BUYING AN AIR CONDITIONER

1. Buy from an honest dealer -- in your community, or one highly recommended and well established.

2. Make sure you get the total price -- including delivery, installation, warranty, etc.

73

3. Make sure all verbal promises are put in writing.

4. See that the guarantee is specific -- spelling out how long it will be effective, and who will honor it.

5. If there is a service contract -- find out if it is at an extra cost, who will provide the service, and exactly what is provided.

6. Don't sign any agreement you do not thoroughly understand.

7. If possible -- ask to see the unit you plan to buy demonstrated, if not, study the instruction manual, so that you know how to use it.

8. Don't be lured into the store with promises of low prices -- only to be switched to a higher priced model -- the advertised model being unobtainable (sold out, not in stock, etc.).

9. When considering repair of a unit:
   a. Get a written itemized estimate (before and after the actual work is done);
   b. Make sure (by checking with another company) that removal of the unit is essential for its repair;
   c. Beware of excessive prices for parts and labor.

HOW TO SPOT WORK-AT-HOME GYPS

1. Be wary of large-profit offers for little or no work.

2. The "for sale" material is not employment, but a product.

3. The investment required is yours (time and money).

4. No salary is ever given by the company.

5. No names are provided for you to check with others, for the benefit of their experience.

6. No leads or market for your product is provided.

LEGISLATION COVERING UNORDERED MERCHANDISE

"Any person receiving unsolicited goods, wares, or

merchandise offerd for sale, but not actually requested or ordered by him orally or in writing, shall be entitled to consider such goods, wares, or merchandise an unconditional gift, and he may use or dispose of the same as he sees fit without any obligation on his part to the sender."

Don't be pressured to pay, by companies who make a practice of mailing unordered merchandise on a "trial basis" in hopes that you will keep it, rather than go through the trouble involved in making a return.

THE ALERT CONSUMER

1. Ask to see the credentials of any sales representative who calls at your door.

2. Check the sales price of services or merchandise with your local merchant.

3. Read and understand everything before you sign a contract:
   a. Did you read the small print?
   b. Is guarantee specific?
   c. Are all blank spaces filled in?
   d. Are all charges itemized?
   e. Are all promises in writing?
   f. Do you have a copy?

4. Where you do not understand the terms of a sales contract, see a lawyer.

5. If the sales price does not include installation and delivery, and you want them included, have the salesman put it in writing in the contract, specifying the type of service, the period during which it will be performed, and the actual date of delivery.

6. Never permit merchandise to be left with you on an "on approval" receipt. The salesman may not return, and you may find yourself billed for an article you neither needed or wanted.

7. Beware of legal "double talk" -- remember that you just can't get something for nothing!

8. If you buy something from a salesman at the door, pay him with a check made out to the company rather than with cash.

9. Purchases bought on the installment plan from a salesman at the door may now be thought over, and canceled (in writing) within three days after signing the initial agreement.

OTHER HINTS -- AVOID DEALERS & MANUFACTURERS WHO FAIL TO:

1. Give prompt attention to complaints -- have no system for receiving, routing, or handling them and evade specific questions along these lines.

2. Honor the guarantee.

3. Write the guarantee in terms which are generally understandable.

4. Replace a "lemon" with a new appliance or refund the purchase price.

5. Take satisfactory direct action -- thereby causing the consumer to pay excessive costs for service and labor in order to repair the appliance.

6. Make necessary repairs -- because parts are not readily available, or because of a manufacturer's delay in authorizing a replacement part, sometimes resulting in spoilage (freezers, etc.).

7. Improve or correct design defects causing repeated breakdown.

8. Provide a free, nominal, or easy way for consumer to return appliances in cases of breakdown.

9. Provide experienced and skilled servicemen whose training is up to date on the latest models.

FOR THOSE DOOR-TO-DOOR SALES

1. Check the salesman's identification -- make sure he rep-

resents the company he claims he does.

2. Make sure the firm is reliable -- check with others with whom he has dealt.

3. Don't be pressured into making an immediate purchase -- compare prices with local merchants and other stores.

4. Know the exact terms and conditions of the sale -- don't sign any agreement you do not understand.

5. Before you sign any contract make sure:
   a. the name and address of the firm and salesman are printed on it;
   b. it has no blank spaces;
   c. all verbal promises which were made are so specified in the contract;
   d. it is specific as to how payments are to be made, delivery date, etc.;
   e. you know the nature of the guarantee (if any).

6. You don't pay cash to a salesman -- pay your bill by check or money order, made out to the company.

7. You have a copy of the contract.

8. Remember that, effective September 1, 1970 in New York State, a law was passed, providing for a three-day cooling-off period to permit a purchaser of a retail installment sales contract from a door-to-door salesman to think over his purchase, change his mind, and cancel the contract, if he chooses, notifying the company in writing within three days of the initial agreement.

Chapter 6

CONCLUSION

The consumer now possesses the right to safety, the right to be informed, the right to choose, and the right to be heard. These rights which President Johnson forecast in 1964 have come to be. They are granted to the consumer by means of legislation, state consumer protection agencies, and the courts.

The process of consumerism has been slow, but through the combined efforts of the state and federal governments, the consumer has the tools with which to make progress. Many local governments have enacted their own consumer legislation and have added still another protective level to the ever growing pyramid of consumer protection.

With all of the available consumer protection agencies, legislation, and other aids, the consumer can, if he wishes, effectively protect his rights. However, the primary responsibility still lies with the individual consumer. He must be aware of his rights and must know how to process his grievances. No area of consumerism is more important than the education of the everyday buyer. He must know his rights in the market place, he must know how to be an intelligent buyer, and he must be aware of the traps and pitfalls he faces each and every day of his consuming life.

This almanac has been but a mere insight into the rights of consumers and it cannot be overemphasized that each consumer must familiarize himself with his particular state statutes, local ordinances, and available private agencies which can help him to be a wise and effective consumer.

A consumer who seeks to educate himself in the ways of the market place and to acquaint himself with his rights and legal protections will by his own individual efforts make a meaningful contribution to the process of fair and equitable dealings between consumers and merchants.

Appendix A

WISCONSIN FRANCHISE LEGISLATION

1971 Senate Bill 784

AN ACT to create 20.185 (3) (a) and chapter 553 of the statutes, relating to regulation of franchise investment by the commissioner of securities, granting rule-making authority, providing penalties and making an appropriation.

The people of the state of Wisconsin, represented in senate and assembly, do enact as follows:

SECTION 1. LEGISLATIVE INTENT. (1) The legislature hereby finds and declares that the widespread sale of franchises is a relatively new form of business which has created numerous problems both from an investment and a business point of view in this state. Prior to the enactment of this act, the sale of franchises was regulated only to the limited extent to which the Wisconsin Uniform Securities Law, chapter 551 of the statutes, applied to such transaction. Wisconsin franchisees have suffered substantial losses where the franchisor or his representative has not provided full and complete information regarding the franchisor-franchisee relationship, the details of the contract between franchisor and franchisee and the prior business experience of the franchisor.

(2) It is the intent of this act to provide each prospective franchisee with the information necessary to make an intelligent decision regarding franchises being offered. Further, it is the intent of this act to prohibit the sale of franchises where such sale would lead to fraud or a likelihood that the franchisor's promises would not be fulfilled, and to protect the franchisee.

SECTION 2. At the appropriate place in the schedule under section 20.005 of the statutes, insert the following amounts for the purposes indicated:

79

(3)   FRANCHISE INVESTMENT REGULATION
  (a)   General program operations   GPR A   50,000   50,000

SECTION 3.   20.185 (3) (a) of the statutes is created to read:

20.185 (3) FRANCHISE INVESTMENT REGULATION. (a) General program operations. The amounts in the schedule for the regulation of franchise investments under ch. 553.

SECTION 4. Chapter 553 of the statutes is created to read:

CHAPTER 553.
WISCONSIN FRANCHISE INVESTMENT LAW.
SUBCHAPTER I.
TITLE AND DEFINITIONS.

553.01 SHORT TITLE. This chapter shall be known and may be cited as the "Wisconsin Franchise Investment Law".

553.03 DEFINITIONS. In this chapter:

(1) "Advertisement" means any circular, prospectus, advertising or other material or any communication by radio, television, pictures or similar means used in connection with a sale or purchase of, or offer to sell or purchase, any franchise.

(2) "Area franchise" means any contract or agreement between a franchisor and a subfranchisor whereby the subfranchisor is granted the right, for consideration given in whole or in part for such right, to sell or negotiate the sale of franchises in the name or on behalf of the franchisor.

(3) "Commissioner" means the commissioner of securities.

(4) (a) "Franchise" means a contract or agreement, either express or implied, whether oral or written, between 2 or more persons which:

1. A franchisee is granted the right to engage in the business of offering, selling or distributing goods or services under a

marketing plan or system prescribed in substantial part by a franchisor; and

2. The operation of the franchisee's business pursuant to such plan or system is substantially associated with the franchisor's business and trademark, service mark, trade name, logotype, advertising or other commercial symbol designating the franchisor or its affiliate; and

3. The franchisee is required to pay, directly or indirectly, a franchise fee.

(b) Unless specifically stated otherwise, "franchise" includes area franchise.

(5) "Franchisee" means a person to whom a franchise is granted.

(6) "Franchisor" means a person who grants a franchise.

(7) "Franchise fee" means any fee or charge that a franchisee or subfranchisor is required to pay or agrees to pay for the right to enter into a business under a franchise agreement, including, but not limited to, any such payment for goods and services. The following shall not be considered the payment of a "franchise fee":

(a) The purchase or agreement to purchase goods at a bona fide wholesale price. The commissioner may issue rules defining wholesale transactions exempt under this paragraph.

(b) The payment of a reasonable service charge to the issuer of a credit card by an establishment accepting or honoring such credit card.

(c) Amounts paid in connection with trading stamp promotions permitted under s. 100.15 by a person issuing trading stamps in connection with the retail sale of merchandise or service.

(d) Any other connection which the commissioner by rule excludes from "franchise fee".

(8) "Fraud and "deceit" are not limited to common law

fraud or deceit.

(9) "Order" means every direction or determination of the commissioner designated an order and made in writing over the signature and seal of the commissioner, except a rule as defined under s. 227.01.

(10) "Publish" means publicly to issue or circulate by newspaper, mail, radio or television, or otherwise to disseminate to the public. Private use of written materials shall not constitute the publication thereof.

(11) (a) "Sale" or "sell" includes every contract or agreement of sale of, contract to sell, or disposition of, a franchise or interest in a franchise for value.

(b) "Offer to sell" includes every attempt to offer to dispose of, or solicitation of an offer to buy, a franchise or interest in a franchise for value. The terms defined in this subsection do not include the renewal or extension of an existing franchise where there is no interruption in the operation of the franchised business by the franchisee.

(c) "Offer to purchase" includes every attempt to offer to acquire, or solicitation of an offer to sell, a franchise or interest in a franchise for value.

(12) "Subfranchisor" means a person to whom an area franchise is granted.

SUBCHAPTER II.
REGISTRATION OF FRANCHISES.

553.21 REGISTRATION REQUIREMENT. (1) No person may sell or offer any franchise in this state unless the offer of the franchise has been registered under this chapter or exempted under s. 553.22, 553.23 or 553.25.

(2) It is unlawful for any franchisor whose franchises are registered under this chapter, or any person in control of or controlled by or under common control with the franchisor, to offer or sell any of the registered franchises in this state in violation of this chapter or any rule under this chapter, or of any

order under this chapter of which he has notice, or if the registration statement relating to the franchise, as of the date of the offer or sale, is incomplete in any material respect or contains any statement which is false or misleading with respect to any material fact. Any person acting under an order or rule under this chapter containing any terms or conditions shall be deemed to have accepted and waived all objections to such terms and conditions.

553.22 EXEMPT PUBLIC OFFERS, SALES AND PURCHASES; BASIS; DISCLOSURE. There shall be exempted from s. 553.21 the offer to sell, the offer to purchase, the sale and the purchase of a franchise if the offeror, seller or purchaser:

(1) Has a net worth on a consolidated basis, according to its most recent audited financial statement, of not less than $5,000,000; or the franchisor has a net worth, according to its most recent audited financial statement, of not less than $3,000,000 and is at least 80% owned by a corporation which has a net worth on a consolidated basis, according to its most recent audited financial statement, of not less than $5,000,000;

(2) Has had at least 25 franchisees conducting the business of the franchisor at 25 locations in this state at all times during the 5-year period immediately preceding the offer or sale; or has conducted business which is the subject of the franchise continuously for not less than 5 years preceding the offer or sale; or if any corporation which owns at least 80% of the franchisor has had at least 25 franchisees conducting the business of the franchisor at 25 locations in this state at all times during the 5-year period immediately preceding the offer or sale;

(3)2Disclosures in writing to each prospective franchisee, at least 48 hours prior to the execution by the prospective franchisee of any binding franchise or other agreement, or at least 48 hours prior to the receipt of any consideration, the following information:

(a) The name of the franchisor, the name under which the franchisor is doing or intends to do business, and the name of any parent or affiliated company that will engage in business transactions with franchisees.

(b) The franchisor's principal business address and the name and address of its agent in this state authorized to receive service of process.

(c) The business form of the franchisor, whether corporate, partnership or otherwise.

(d) The business experience of the franchisor, including the length of time the franchisor has conducted a business of the type to be operated by the franchisees, has granted franchises for such business and has granted franchises in other lines of business.

(e) A copy of the typical franchise contract or agreement proposed for use or in use in this state.

(f) A statement of the franchise fee charged, the proposed application of the proceeds of such fee by the franchisor, and the formula by which the amount of the fee is determined if the fee is not the same in all cases.

(g) A statement describing any payments or fees other than franchise fees that the franchisee or subfranchisor is required to pay to the franchisor, including royalties and payments or fees which the franchisor collects in whole or in part on behalf of a third part.

(h) A statement of the conditions under which the franchise agreement or portions thereof may be assigned, terminated or renewal refused, or the franchise repurchased at the option of the franchisor.

(i) A statement as to whether, by the terms of the franchise agreement or by other device or practice, the franchisee or subfranchisor is required to purchase from the franchisor or his designee services, supplies, products, fixtures or other goods relating to the establishment or operation of the franchise business, together with a description thereof as to kind and amount.

(j) A statement as to whether, by the terms of the franchise agreement or other device or practice, the franchisee is limited in the goods or services offered by him to his customers.

(k) A statement of the terms and conditions of any financing arrangements when offered directly or indirectly by the franchisor or his agent or affiliate.

(l) A statement of any past or present practice or of any intent of the franchisor to sell, assign or discount to a third party any note, contract or other obligation of the franchisee or subfranchisor in whole or in part.

(m) If any statement of estimated or projected franchisee earnings is used, a statement of such estimation or projection and the data upon which it is based.

(n) A statement as to whether franchisees or subfranchisors receive an exclusive area or territory and, if so, a graphic representation thereof; and

(4) Files with the commissioner at least 10 days prior to the offer, sale or purchase of a franchise in this state under this section a copy of the information to be distributed to each prospective franchisee under sub. (3) together with the consent to service of process as specified in s. 553.27 (10).

553.23 PRIVATE FRANCHISEE AND SUBFRANCHISOR SALES EXEMPTED. The offer or sale of a franchise by a franchisee for his own account or the offer or sale of the entire area franchise owned by a subfranchisor for his own account is exempted from s. 553.21 if the sale is not effected by or through a franchisor. Disclosure as required by s. 553.22 (3) shall be made in all such transfers as a condition of this exemption except where a bona fide attempt to obtain information necessary for such disclosure has been made by the seller and the source from which the information is available refuses to produce the information. A sale is not effected by or through a franchisor merely because a franchisor has a right to approve or disapprove a different franchisee.

553.24 EXEMPTION PROCEEDINGS. (1) The commissioner may by order deny or revoke any exemption specified in s. 553.22 or 553.23 with respect to the offer or sale of a specific franchise. No such order may be entered without appropriate prior notice to all interested parties, opportunity for hearing, and written findings of fact and conclusions of law, except that the commissioner may by order summarily deny or revoke any of the specified exemptions pending final determination of any proceeding under this section. Upon the entry of a summary order, the commissioner shall promptly notify all interested parties that it has been entered and the reasons therefore and that within 15 days of the receipt of a written request the matter will be set down for hearing. If no hearing is requested and none is ordered by the commissioner, the order will remain in effect until it is modified or vacated by the commissioner. If a hearing is requested or ordered, the commissioner, after notice of and opportunity for hearing to all interested persons, may modify or vacate the order or extend it until final determination. No order under this section may operate retroactively. No person may be considered to have violated s. 553.21 by reason of any offer or sale effected after the entry of an order under this section if he sustains the burden of proof that he did not know, and in the exercise of reasonable care would not have known, of the order.

(2) In any proceeding under this chapter, the burden of proving an exemption or an exception from a definition is upon the person claiming it.

553.25 EXEMPTION BY COMMISSIONER. There shall be exempted from s. 553.21 any other transaction which the commissioner by rule exempts as not being comprehended within the purposes of this chapter and the registration of which he finds is not necessary or appropriate in the public interest or for the protection of investors.

553.26 APPLICATION FOR REGISTRATION. The application for registration of an offer shall be filed with the commissioner and shall contain the following:

(1) The name of the franchisor, the name under which the franchisor is doing or intends to do business and the name of any parent or affiliated company that will engage in business transactions with franchisees.

(2) The franchisor's principal business address and the name and address of its agent in this state authorized to receive service of process.

(3) The business form of the franchisor, whether corporate,

partnership or otherwise.

(4) Such information concerning the identity and business experience of persons affiliated with the franchisor, as the commissioner may by rule prescribe.

(5) (a) A statement whether any person identified in the application for registration:

1. Has been convicted of a felony, or pleaded nolo contendere to a felony charge, or held liable in a civil action by final judgment if such felony or civil action involved fraud, embezzlement, fraudulent conversion or misappropriation of property; or

2. Is subject to any currently effective order of the U.S. securities and exchange commission or the securities administrator of any state denying registration to or revoking or suspending the registration of such person as a securities broker or dealer or investment advisor or is subject to any currently effective order of any national securities association or national securities exchange, as defined in the federal securities and exchange act of 1934, suspending or expelling such person from membership in such association or exchange; or

3. Is subject to any currently effective order or ruling of the federal trade commission; or

4. Is subject to any currently effective injunctive or restrictive order relating to business activity as a result of an action brought by any public agency or department, including, without limitation, actions affecting a license as a real estate broker or salesman.

(b) Such statement shall set forth the court, date of conviction or judgment, any penalty imposed or damages assessed, or the date, nature and issuer of such order.

(6) The length of time the franchisor has conducted a business of the type to be operated by the franchisees, has granted franchises for such business, and has granted franchises in other lines of business.

(7) A recent financial statement of the franchisor, together

with a statement of any material changes in the financial condition of the franchisor from the date thereof. The commissioner may by rule or order prescribe:

(a) The form and content of financial statements required under this subsection;

(b) The circumstances under which consolidated financial statements shall be filed; and

(c) The circumstances under which financial statements shall be audited by independent certified public accountants or public accountants.

(8) A copy of the typical franchise contract or agreement proposed for use or in use in this state.

(9) A statement of the franchise fee charged, the proposed application of the proceeds of such fee by the franchisor and the formula by which the amount of the fee is determined if the fee is not the same in all cases.

(10) A statement describing any payments or fees other than franchise fees that the franchisee or subfranchisor is required to pay to the franchisor, including royalties and payments or fees which the franchisor collects in whole or in part on behalf of a third party.

(11) A statement of the conditions under which the franchise agreement or portions thereof may be assigned, terminated or renewal refused, or the franchise repurchased at the option of the franchisor.

(12) A statement as to whether, by the terms of the franchise agreement or by other device or practice, the franchisee or subfranchisor is required to purchase from the franchisor or his designee services, supplies, products, fixtures or other goods relating to the establishment or operation of the franchise business, together with a description thereof as to kind and amount.

(13) A statement as to whether, by the terms of the franchise agreement or other device or practice, the franchisee

is limited in the goods or services offered by him to his customers.

(14) A statement of the terms and conditions of any financing arrangements when offered directly or indirectly by the franchisor or his agent or affiliate.

(15) A statement of any past or present practice or of any intent of the franchisor to sell, assign or discount to a third party any note, contract or other obligation of the franchisee or subfranchisor in whole or in part.

(16) A copy of any statement of estimated or projected franchisee earnings prepared for presentation to prospective franchisees or subfranchisors, or other persons, together with a statement setting forth the data upon which such estimation or projection is based.

(17) A statement of any compensation or other benefit given or promised to a public figure arising, in whole or in part, from the use of the public figure in the name or symbol of the franchise or the indorsement or recommendation of the franchise by the public figure in advertisements.

(18) A statement of the number of franchises presently operating and proposed to be sold, as may be required by rule of the commissioner.

(19) A statement as to whether franchisees or subfranchisors receive an exclusive area or territory and, if so, a graphic representation thereof.

(20) Other information related to the application as the commissioner may reasonably require.

(21) Other information the franchisor may desire to present.

(22) If the person filing the application for registration is a subfranchisor, the application shall also include the same information concerning the subfranchisor as is required from the franchisor pursuant to this section.

553.27 GENERAL REGISTRATION PROVISIONS. (1) Applications for registration, registration renewal statements and amendments thereto, shall be signed and notarized by the franchisor or by the subfranchisor.

(2) If the commissioner finds that the applicant has failed to demonstrate that adequate financial arrangements have been made to fulfill obligation to provide real estate, improvements, equipment, inventory, training or other items included in the offering, the commissioner may by rule or order require the escrow of franchise fees and other funds paid by the franchisee or subfranchisor until no later than the time of opening of the franchise business, or, at the option of the franchisor, the furnishing of a surety bond as provided by rule of the commissioner, if he finds that such requirement is necessary and appropriate to protect prospective franchisees or subfranchisors.

(3) The application for registration shall be accompanied by a proposed offering prospectus, which shall contain the material information set forth in the application for registration, as specified by rule of the commissioner, and such additional disclosures as the commissioner may require. The prospectus shall recite in bold type of not less than 10-point type that registration does not constitute approval recommendation or indorsement by the commissioner.

(4) It is unlawful to sell any franchise in this state which is subject to registration under this chapter without first providing to the prospective franchisee, at least 48 hours prior to the execution by the prospective franchisee of any binding franchise or other agreement, or at least 48 hours prior to the receipt of any consideration, whichever occurs first, a copy of the prospectus, together with a copy of all proposed agreements relating to the sale of the franchise.

(5) Every franchisor or subfranchisor offering franchises for sale in this state shall at all times keep and maintain a complete set of books, records and accounts of such sales.

(6) The commissioner may accept and act upon the opinions, appraisals and reports of any engineers, appraisers or other experts which may be presented by an applicant or any interested party, on any question of fact concerning or affecting the fran-

chises proposed to be offered and sold. In lieu of, or in addition to, such opinions, appraisals and reports, the commissioner may have any or all matters concerning or affecting such franchises investigated, appraised, passed upon and certified to him by engineers, appraisers or other experts selected by him.

(7) Any document filed under this chapter or ch. 551 may be incorporated by reference in a subsequent application filed under this chapter if it was filed within 2 years prior to the filing of such application, or is otherwise available in the files of the commissioner, to the extent that the document is currently accurate.

(8) The registration statement shall consist of a circular containing those items required by s. 553.26 to be disclosed to investors together with other documents which the commissioner by rule prescribes.

(9) Neither the fact that an application for registration under this chapter has been filed, nor the fact that such registration has become effective constitutes a finding by the commissioner that any document filed under this chapter is true, complete or not misleading. Neither any such fact nor the fact that an exemption is available for a transaction means that the commissioner has passed in any way upon the merits or qualifications of, or recommended or given approval to, any person, franchise or transaction. No person may make or cause to be made to any prospective purchaser or offeree any representation inconsistent with this subsection.

(10) Every applicant for registration of an offer to sell franchises under this chapter shall file with the commissioner, in such forms as he by rule prescribes, an irrevocable consent appointing the commissioner or his successor in office to be his attorney to receive service of any lawful process in any civil action against him or his successor, executor or administrator, which arises under this chapter or any rule or order hereunder after the consent has been filed, with the same force and validity as if served personally on the person filing the consent. A person who has filed such a consent in connection with a previous registration under this chapter need not file another. Service may be made by leaving a copy of the process in the office of the commissioner but it is not effective unless the plaintiff, who may be the commissioner in action instituted by him, forthwith

sends notice of the service and a copy of the process by registered or certified mail to the defendant or respondent at his last address on file with the commissioner, and the plaintiff's affidavit of compliance with the subsection is filed in the case on or before the return day of the process, if any, or with such further time as the court allows.

553.28 DENIAL, SUSPENSION OR REVOCATION OF REGISTRATIONS OR EXEMPTIONS. (1) The commissioner may summarily issue a stop order denying the effectiveness of or suspending or revoking effectiveness of any registration statement or revoking any exemption in accordance with s. 553.24 if he finds any of the following:

(a) That there has been a failure to comply with this chapter or the rules of the commissioner pertaining thereto.

(b) That the offer, purchase or sale of the franchise would constitute misrepresentation to or deceit or fraud upon purchasers thereof, or has worked or tended to work a fraud upon purchasers or would so operate.

(c) That any person in this state is engaging or about to engage in false, fraudulent or deceptive practices in connection with the offer, purchase or sale of a franchise in this state.

(d) That any person identified in an application for registration has been convicted of an offence under s. 553.26 (5), or is subject to an order, or has had a civil judgment entered against him as described in s. 553.26 (5), and the involvement of such person in the same or management of the franchise creates an unreasonable risk to prospective franchisees.

(e) That the applicant or registrant has failed to pay the proper filing fee; but the commissioner may enter only a denial order under this paragraph and he shall vacate any such order when the deficiency has been corrected.

(f) That advertising prohibited by s. 553.53 has been used in connection with the offer, purchase or sale of franchises.

(g) That the financial condition of the franchisor affects or would affect the ability of the franchisor to fulfill obligations under the franchise agreement.

(h) That the franchisor's enterprise or method of business includes or would include activities which are illegal where performed.

(2) (a) The commissioner may issue a summary order denying, postponing, suspending or revoking the effectiveness of the registration pending final determination of any proceeding under this section. Upon the entry of the order, the commissioner shall promptly notify each person specified in par. (b) that it has been entered and the reasons therefor and that within 15 days after the receipt of a written request the matter will be set down for hearing. If no hearing is requested and none is ordered by the commissioner, the order will remain in effect until it is modified or vacated by the commissioner. If a hearing is requested or ordered, the commissioner, after notice of and opportunity for hearing to each person specified in par. (b), may modify or vacate the order or extend it until final determination.

(b) No stop order may be entered under this section except under par. (a) without appropriate prior notice to the applicant or registrant and the person on whose behalf the franchise is to be or has been offered; opportunity for hearing; and written findings of fact and conclusions of law.

(3) The commissioner may vacate or modify an order entered under s. 553.24 or this section if he finds that the conditions which prompted its entry have changed or that it is otherwise in the public interest to do so.

553.29 EFFECTIVE DATE AND DURATION OF REGISTRATION. (1) If no stop order under s. 553.28 is in effect, registration of the offer of franchises becomes effective at 12 m., of the 15th business day after the filing of the application for registration or the last amendment thereto, or at such earlier time as the commissioner determines.

(2) A franchise offering shall be duly registered for a period of one year from the effective date of the registration, unless the commissioner by order or rule specifies a different period.

(3) Registration of franchises shall be by order of the commissioner, but the failure to issue an order shall not delay the effectiveness of a registration statement meeting the requirements of s. 553.26.

553.30 REGISTRATION STATEMENT RENEWAL. (1) The registration statement may be renewed for additional periods of one year each, unless the commissioner by rule or order specifies a different period, by submitting to the commissioner a registration renewal statement no later than 15 business days prior to the expiration of the registration unless such period is waived by order of the commissioner. If no stop order or other order under s. 553.28 is in effect, renewal of the registration statement becomes effective on the day on which the prior registration statement expires or at such earlier time as the commissioner determines.

(2) The registration renewal statement shall be in the form and content prescribed by the commissioner, and shall be accompanied by 2 copies of the proposed offering prospectus. Each such registration renewal statement shall be accompanied by the fee prescribed in s. 553.72.

553.31 AMENDMENT TO REGISTRATION STATEMENT. (1) A franchisor shall within 30 days after the happening of any material event affecting a registered franchise notify the commissioner in writing, by an application to amend the registration statement, of any material change in the information contained in the application as originally submitted, amended or renewed. The commissioner may by rule further define what shall be considered a material change for such purposes, and the circumstances under which a revised offering prospectus must accompany such application.

(2) An amendment to an application filed after the effective date of the registration of the sale of franchises, if such amendment is approved by the commissioner, shall become effective on such date as the commissioner determines, having due regard for the public interest and the protection of franchisees.

SUBCHAPTER III.
FRAUDULENT AND PROHIBITED PRACTICES.

553.41 FRAUDULENT AND PROHIBITED PRACTICES. (1)

No person may make or cause to be made, in any document filed with the commissioner or in any proceeding under this chapter, any statement which is, at the time and in the light of the circumstances under which it is made, false or misleading in any material respect or, in connection with any statement required to be made under s. 553.31 (1), omit to state a material fact necessary in order to make the statement made, in the light of the circumstances under which they are made, not misleading.

(2) No person may violate any order of the commissioner or condition therein of which he has notice.

(3) No person may offer, purchase or sell a franchise in this state by means of any written or oral communication not included in sub. (1) which includes an untrue statement of a material fact or omits to state a material fact necessary in order to make the statements made, in the light of the circumstances under which they were made, not misleading.

(4) No person may make any untrue statement of a material fact in any statement required to be disclosed in writing in a timely manner pursuant to s. 553.22, 553.23 or 553.27 or omit to state in any such statement any material fact which is required to be stated therein.

(5) No person may wilfully represent to any prospective purchaser or seller of a franchise in this state that the filing of a franchise registration application or the registration of a franchise constitutes a finding by the commissioner that any document filed under this chapter is true, complete, and not misleading, or in relation to an exemption or exception, that the commissioner has passed in any way upon the merits of any franchise or wilfully represent in a similar manner that a franchise is registered or exempted when in fact, such is not the case.

SUBCHAPTER IV.
ENFORCEMENT AND GENERAL PROVISIONS.

553.51 CIVIL LIABILITY; OFFER OR SALE IN VIOLATION. (1) Any person who offers, purchases or sells a franchise in violation of s. 553.21 or 553.41 (1), (2), (4) or (5) shall be liable to the franchisee or subfranchisor, who may bring an action for rescission, unless, in the case of a violation of s. 553.41 (1), (2), (4) or (5), the defendant proves that the plaintiff knew the facts concerning the untruth or omission, or that the defendant exercised reasonable care and did not know, or, if he had exercised reasonable care, would not have known, of the untruth or omission.

(2) Any person who violates s. 553.41 (3) shall be liable to any person not knowing or having cause to believe that such statement was false or misleading who, while relying upon such statement, shall have sold or purchased a franchise, for damages, unless the defendant proves that the plaintiff knew the facts concerning the untruth or omission or that the defendant exercised reasonable care and did not know, or if he had exercised reasonable care would not have known, of the untruth or omission.

(3) Every person who directly or indirectly controls a person liable under sub. (1) or (2), every partner in a firm so liable, every principal executive officer or director of a corporation so liable, every person occupying a similar status or performing similar functions and every employe of a person so liable who materially aids in the act or transaction constituting the violation is also liable jointly and severally with and to the same extent as such person, unless the person who would otherwise be liable hereunder had no knowledge of or reasonable grounds to believe in the existence of the facts by reason of which the liability is alleged to exist.

(4) No action may be maintained to enforce any liability under this section unless brought before the expiration of 3 years after the act or transaction constituting the violation upon which the liability is based, the expiration of one year after the discovery by the plaintiff of the fact constituting the violation, or 90 days after delivery to the franchisee of a written notice disclosing any violation of s. 553.21 or 553.41, which notice shall be approved as to form by the commissioner, whichever first expires.

(5) The rights and remedies under this chapter are in addition to any other rights or remedies that may exist at law or in equity.

553.52 CRIMINAL PENALTIES. (1) Any person who

wilfully violates any provision of this chapter except s. 553.41 (1), or any rule under this chapter, or any order of which he has notice, or who violates s. 553.41 (1) knowing or having reasonable cause to believe either that the statement made was false or misleading in any material respect or that the failure to report a material event under s. 553.31 (1) was false or misleading in any material respect, may be fined not more than $5,000 or imprisoned not more than 5 years or both. Each of the acts specified shall constitute a separate offense and a prosecution or conviction for any one of such offenses shall not bar prosecution or conviction for any other offense. No indictment or information may be returned under this chapter more than 6 years after the alleged violation.

(2) Any person who employs, directly or indirectly, any device, scheme or artifice to defraud in connection with the offer or sale of any franchise or engages, directly or indirectly, in any act, practice, or course of business which operates or would operate as a fraud or deceit upon any person in connection with the offer, purchase or sale of any franchise shall be fined not more than $5,000 or imprisoned not more than 5 years, or both.

(3) Nothing in this section limits the power of the state to punish any person for any conduct which constitutes a crime under any other statute.

553.53 ADVERTISING. No person may publish, distribute or use in this state any advertisement offering to sell or to purchase a franchise unless 2 true copies of the advertisement have been filed in the office of the commissioner at least 5 days prior to the first publication, distribution or use thereof or such shorter period as the commissioner by rule or order may allow, or unless the advertisement has been exempted from this section by rule of the commissioner. The commissioner may by rule or order prohibit the use of advertising deemed false, fraudulent, misleading or deceptive.

553.54 INJUNCTIONS. (1) The department of justice or any district attorney, upon informing the department of justice, may commence an action in circuit court in the name of the state to restrain by temporary or permanent injunction any act or practice constitution a violation of this chapter or any rule or order hereunder. The commissioner may refer such eveidence as is available concerning any violation to the district attorney of the county in which the violation occurred or to the attorney general who may institute proceedings under this section.

(2) (a) The court may, prior to the entry of final judgment, make such orders or judgments as may be necessary to restore to any person any pecuniary loss suffered because of the acts or practices involved in the action if proof thereof is submitted to the satisfaction of the court. Such orders or judgments shall not provide restoration of any pecuniary loss to persons for whom such recovery was sought where the defendant in the action can establish that such persons were in possession of knowledge such as would defeat recovery by them in a private civil action under s. 553.51 (1) or (2).

(b) Upon a proper showing, a temporary or permanent injunction or restraining order shall be granted and a receiver or conservator may be appointed for the defendant or the defendant's assests. The court shall not require the department of justice to post a bond.

(3) The department of justice may subpoena persons, administer oaths, take testimony, require the production of books and other documents and may request the commissioner to exercise his authority under s. 553.53 to aid in the investigation of alleged violations of this chapter. If a person fails to obey any subpoena issued by the department of justice, he may be coerced under s. 885.12, except that no person shall be required to furnish any testimony or evidence under this subsection which might tend to incriminate him.

(4) In lieu of instituting or continuing an action pursuant to this section, the commissioner or the department of justice may accept a written assurance of discontinuance of any act or practice alleged to be a violation of this chapter from the person who has engaged in such act or practice. The acceptance of such assurance by either the commissioner or the department shall be deemed acceptance by other state officials if the terms of the assurance so provide. An assurance entered into pursuant to this subsection shall not be considered evidence of a violation of this chapter, however, a violation of such an assurance constitutes a violation of this chapter and shall be subject to all penalties and remedies provided therefor.

553.55 INVESTIGATIONS AND SUBPOENAS. (1) The commissioner may make such public or private investigations within or outside of this state as he deems necessary to determine whether any person has violated or is about to violate this chapter or any rule or order hereunder or to aid in the enforcement of this chapter or in the prescribing of rules and forms hereunder, and publish information concerning the violation of this chapter or any rule or order hereunder.

(2) For the purpose of any investigation or proceeding under this chapter, the commissioner or any officer designated by him may administer oaths and affirmations, subpoena witnesses, compel their attendance, take evidence and require the production of any books, papers, correspondence, memoranda, agreements or other documents or records which the commissioner deems relevant or material to the inquiry. Failure to obey a subpoena or give evidence may be dealt with under s. 885.12.

(3) No person is excused from attending and testifying or from producing any document or record before the commissioner, or in obedience to the subpoena of the commissioner or any officer designated by him, or in any proceeding instituted by the commissioner, on the ground that the testimony or evidence required of him may tend to incriminate him or subject him to a penalty or forfeiture; but no individual may be prosecuted or subjected to any penalty or forfeiture for or on account of any transaction, matter or thing concerning which he is compelled, after claiming his privilege against self-incrimination, to testify or produce evidence, except that the individual testifying is not exempt from prosecution and punishment for perjury or contempt committed in testifying.

553.56 HEARINGS AND JUDICIAL REVIEW. (1) Within 30 days after any order issued under s. 553.24 or 553.28 has become effective without a hearing, any interested party may apply to the commissioner for a hearing in respect to any matters determined by the order, and a hearing shall be held within 15 days after the application is filed. After the hearing the commissioner may affirm, modify or vacate the order as he deems appropriate.

(2) Within 30 days after any order has become effective

after a hearing, any interested party may apply to the commissioner for a rehearing. The commissioner may grant and hold a rehearing if in his judgment sufficient reasons therefor appear. After rehearing, the commissioner may affirm, vacate or modify the order, and any order vacating or modifying the original order shall have the same effect as an original order. Failure to grant an application for rehearing within 30 days from the date of the filing shall constitute a denial; and failure, within 15 days after the conclusion of a rehearing, to issue an order affirming, vacating or modifying the original order shall constitute an affirmation of the original order.

(3) Hearings and rehearings shall be public unless the commissioner grants a request joined in by all parties that the hearing be conducted privately.

(4) Orders and other official acts of the commissioner shall be subject to judicial review under ch. 227 but orders originally entered without a hearing under s. 553.24 or 553.28 may be reviewed only if the party seeking review has requested a hearing within the time provided by sub. (1).

553.57 ENFORCEMENT OF CRIMINAL PENALTIES. The commissioner may refer such evidence as is available concerning any violation of this chapter or of any rule or order hereunder to the district attorney of the county in which the violation occurred, or to the attorney general, who may, with or without any reference, institute the appropriate criminal proceedings under this chapter.

553.58 RULES, FORMS AND ORDERS. (1) The commissioner may make, amend and rescind any rules, forms and orders that are necessary to carry out this chapter, including rules and forms governing registration statements, applications and reports, defining any terms, whether or not used in this chapter, insofar as the definitions are not inconsistent with this chapter. The commissioner may define by rule false, fraudulent or deceptive practices in the offer and sale of franchises. The commissioner may also adopt rules with regard to advertising utilized in connection with exempt sales under s. 553.22 or 553.23 and which need not be filed under s. 553.53. For the purpose of rules and forms, the commissioner may classify franchises, persons and matters within his jurisdiction, and prescribe different requirements for different classes. Rules shall be made and published and all administrative procedures, including hearings under s. 553.56 and issuance of orders, shall be in accordance with chapter 227.

(2) No rule, form or order may be made, amended or rescinded unless the commissioner finds that the action is necessary or appropriate in the public interest and for the protection of investors. In prescribing rules and forms the commissioner may cooperate with official administrators of other states.

(3) The commissioner may by rule or order prescribe the form and content of financial statements required under this chapter, the circumstances under which consolidated financial statements shall be filed, and whether any required financial statements shall be certified by independent or certified public accountants. All financial statements shall be prepared in accordance with generally accepted accounting practices unless otherwise permitted by rule or order.

(4) No provision of this chapter imposing any liability applies to any act done or omitted in good faith in conformity with any rule, form or order of the commissioner, notwithstanding that the rule, form or order may later be amended or rescinded or be determined to be invalid for any reason.

(5) All orders shall take effect when made and filed or at such later time as the commissioner prescribes, and the commissioner shall, upon making and filing such order, forthwith send a copy thereof to every person to whom such order relates by registered mail to his last-known address as it appears on the records of the office of the commissioner and such mailing shall constitute notice thereof.

553.59 SCOPE OF CHAPTER. (1) The provisions of this chapter concerning sales and offers to sell apply when a sale or offer to sell is made in this state or when an offer to purchase is made and accepted in this state. The provisions concerning purchases and offers to purchase apply when a purchase or offer to purchase is made in this state or an offer to sell is made and accepted in this state.

(2) For the purpose of this section, an offer to sell or to purchase is made in this state, whether or not either party is then present in this state, when the offer originates from the state or is directed by the offeror to this state and received by the offeree in this state, but for the purpose of s. 553.21, an offer to sell which is not directed to or received by the offeree in this state is not made in this state.

(3) For the purpose of this section, an offer to purchase or to sell is accepted in this state when acceptance is communicated to the offeror in this state, and has not previously been communicated to the offeror, orally or in writing, outside this state; and acceptance is communicated to the offeror in this state, whether or not either party is then present in this state, when the offeree directs it to the offeror in this state reasonably believing the offeror to be in this state and it is received by the offeror in this state.

(4) An offer to sell or to purchase is not made in this state when the publisher circulates or there is circulated on his behalf in this state any bona fide newspaper or other publication of general, regular and paid circulation which is not published in this state, or a radio or television program originating outside this state is received in this state.

SUBCHAPTER V.
ADMINISTRATION.

553.71 ADMINISTRATION. (1) This chapter shall be administered by the commissioner of securities and by the department of justice when exercising its authority under s. 553.54.

(2) It is unlawful for the commissioner or any of his officers or employes to use for personal benefit any information which is filed with or obtained by the commissioner and which is not generally available to the public. Nothing in this chapter authorizes the commissioner or any of his officers or employes to disclose any confidential information except among themselves or to other securities administrators or regulatory authorities or when necessary or appropriate in a proceeding or investigation under this chapter. No provision of this chapter either creates or derogates from any privilege

which exists at common law or otherwise when documentary or other evidence is sought under a subpoena directed to the commissioner or any of his officers or employes.

553.72 FEES. The commissioner shall charge and collect the fees fixed by this section.

(1) The fee for filing an application for registration of the sale of franchises under s. 553.26 is $200.

(2) The fee for filing an application for renewal of a registration under s. 553.30 is $100.

(3) The fee for filing an amendment to the application filed under s. 553.31 is $50.

(4) The expenses reasonably attributable to the examination of any matter arising under this chapter shall be charged to the applicant or registrant involved, but the expenses so charged shall not exceed such maximum amounts as the commissioner by rule prescribes.

553.73 SERVICE OF PROCESS. When any person, including any nonresident of this state, engages in conduct prohibited or made actionable by this chapter or any rule or order hereunder, whether or not he has filed a consent to service of process under s. 553.27 (10), and personal jurisdiction over him cannot otherwise be obtained in this state, that conduct shall be considered equivalent to his appointment of the commissioner or his successor in office to be his attorney to receive service of any lawful process in any noncriminal suit, action or proceeding against him or his successor, executor or administrator which grows out of that conduct and which is brought under this law or any rule or order hereunder, with the same force and validity as if served on him personally. Service may be made by leaving a copy of the process in the office of the commissioner, but it is not effective unless the plaintiff, who may be the commissioner in a suit, action or proceeding instituted by him, forthwith sends notice of the service and a copy of the process by registered or certified mail to the defendant or respondent at his last-known address or takes other steps which are reasonably calculated to give actual notice, and the plaintiff's affidavit of compliance with this section is filed in the case

103

on or before the return day of the process, if any, or within such further time as the court allows.

553.74 PUBLIC RECORDS. (1) All applications, reports and other papers and documents filed with the commissioner under this chapter shall be open to public inspection in accordance with rules prescribed by the commissioner. The commissioner may publish any information filed with him or obtained by him, if, in the judgment of the commissioner, such action is in the public interest. No provision of this chapter authorizes the commissioner or any of his assistants, clerks or deputies to disclose any information withheld from public inspection except among themselves or when necessary or appropriate in a proceeding or investigation under this chapter or to other federal or state regulatory agencies. No provision of this chapter either creates or derogates from any privilege which exists at common law or otherwise when documentary or other evidence is sought under a subpoena directed to the commissioner or any of his assistants, clerks or deputies.

(2) It is unlawful for the commissioner or any of his assistants, clerks or deputies or employes to use for personal benefit any information which is filed with or obtained by the commissioner and which is not then generally available to the public.

553.75 ADMINISTRATIVE FILES AND OPINIONS. (1) A document is filed when it is received by the commissioner.

(2) The commissioner shall keep a register of all filings which are or have ever been effective under this chapter and predecessor laws and all denial, suspension or revocation orders which have been entered under this chapter. The register shall be open for public inspection.

(3) The information contained in or filed with any registration statement, application or report shall be made available to the public in accordance with rules prescribed by the commissioner.

(4) The commissioner upon request shall furnish to any person at a reasonable charge photostatic or other copies, certified under his seal of office, if certification is requested,

of any entry in the register or any order or other document on file in his office. Any copy so certified is admissible in evidence under s. 889.18.

(5) The commissioner may honor requests from interested persons for interpretative opinions.

553.76 WAIVERS VOID. Any condition, stipulation or provision purporting to bind any person acquiring any franchise to waive compliance with any provision of this chapter or any rule or order hereunder is void.

553.77 SAVING PROVISION. Prior law exclusively governs all suits, actions, prosecutions or proceedings which are pending or may be initiated on the basis of facts or circumstances occurring before July 1, 1972.

553.78 PREEMPTION. This chapter shall not preempt the administration of ch. 96, 100, 133, 168, 176 or 218. False, fraudulent and deceptive practices in connection with the offer, purchase or sale of a franchise defined by rule of the commissioner under s. 553.58 (1) may also constitute unfair methods of competition in business or unfair trade practices in business under s. 100.20 (1) or fraudulent advertising under s. 100.18.

SECTION 5. EFFECTIVE DATE OF CERTAIN APPLICA-TIONS. With respect to any application for registration or the last amendment thereto filed between July 1, 1972, and September 15, 1972, if no stop order under section 553.28 of the statutes is in effect, registration becomes effective on October 15, 1972; with respect to any application filed after September 15, 1972, and before November 10, 1972, if no stop order under section 553.28 of the statutes is in effect, registration becomes effective on December 1, 1972, or the 15th business day after the filing, whichever is later, or at such earlier time as the commissioner determines.

SECTION 6. PROGRAM RESPONSIBILITIES. At the appropriate place in the list of program responsibilities specified for the commissioner of securities under section 15.851 of the statutes, insert reference to chapter "553".

SECTION 7. EFFECTIVE DATE. This act shall take effect July 1, 1972.

OHIO CONSUMER LEGISLATION

(Amended Substitute House Bill No. 350)

SECTION 1. That sections 1309.47, 1317.01, 1317.06, and 1317.07 be amended, and sections 1317.031, 1317.071, 1317.12, 1317.13, 1317.14, and 1317.16 of the Revised Code be enacted to read as follows:

Sec. 1309.47. (A) A secured party after default may sell, lease, or otherwise dispose of any or all of the collateral in its then condition or following any commercially reasonable preparation or processing. Any sale of goods is subject to sections 1302.01 to 1302.98, of the Revised Code. The proceeds of disposition shall be applied in the order following to:

(1) the reasonable expenses of retaking, holding, preparing for sale, selling, and the like.

(2) the satisfaction of indebtedness secured by the security interest under which the disposition is made;

(3) the satisfaction of indebtedness secured by any subordinate security interest in the collateral if written notification of demand therefor is received before distribution of the proceeds is completed. If requested by the secured party, the holder of a subordinate security interest must seasonably furnish reasonable proof of his interest, and unless he does so, the secured party need not comply with his demand.

(B) If the security interest secures an indebtedness, the secured party must account to the debtor for any surplus, and, unless otherwise agreed, the debtor is liable for any deficiency. But if the underlying transaction was a sale of accounts, contract rights, or chattel paper, the debtor is entitled to any surplus or is liable for any deficiency only if the security agreement so provides.

(C) Disposition of the collateral may be by public or

private proceedings and may be made by way of one or more contracts. Sale or other disposition may be as a unit or in parcels and at any time and place and on any terms but every aspect of the disposition including the method, manner, time, place, and terms must be commercially reasonable. Unless collateral is perishable or threatens to decline speedily in value or is of a type customarily sold on a recognized market, reasonable notification of the time and place of any public sale or reasonable notification of the time after which any private sale or other intended disposition is to be made shall be sent by the secured party to the debtor, and except in the case of consumer goods to any other person who has a security interest in the collateral and who has duly filed a financing statement indexed in the name of the debtor in this state or who is known by the secured party to have a security interest in the collateral. The secured party may buy at any public sale and if the collateral is of a type customarily sold in a recognized market or is of a type which is the subject of widely distributed standard price quotations he may buy at private sale.

(D) When collateral is disposed of by a secured party after default, the disposition transfers to a purchaser for value all of the debtor's rights therein, discharges the security interest under which it is made and any security interest or lien subordinate thereto. The purchaser takes free of all such rights and interests even though the secured party fails to comply with the requirements of sections 1309.44 to 1309.50, of the Revised Code or of any judicial proceedings.

(1) in the case of a public sale, if the purchaser has no knowledge of any defects in the sale and if he does not buy in collusion with the secured party, other bidders, or the person conducting the sale; or

(2) in any other case, if the purchaser acts in good faith.

(E) A person who is liable to a secured party under a guaranty, indorsement, repurchase agreement, or the like and who receives a transfer of collateral from the secured party or is subrogated to his rights has thereafter the rights and duties of the secured party. Such a transfer of collateral is not a sale or disposition of the collateral under sections 1309.01 to 1309.50 of the Revised Code.

(F) "Buyer" means a person who buys or agrees to buy goods or any legal successor in interest of such person.

(G) "Retail buyer" means a buyer who is a party to a retail installment sale, or any legal successor in interest of such person.

(H) "Seller" means a person who sells or agrees to sell goods.

(I) "Retail seller" means a seller who is a party to a retail installment sale.

(J) "Holder of the retail installment contract" means any person to whom the money owed by the retail buyer on the retail installment contract has been paid.

(K) "Cash price" means the price measured in dollars, agreed upon in good faith by the parties as the price at which the specific goods which are the subject matter of any retail installment sale would be sold if such sale were a sale for cash to be paid upon delivery instead of a retail installment sale.

(L) "Retail installment contract" means any written instrument which is executed in connection with any retail installment sale and is required by section 1317.02 of the Revised Code or is authorized by section 1317.03 of the Revised Code, and includes all such instruments executed in connection with any retail installment sale.

(M) "Contract for sale" and "sale" have the same meaning as they are defined in section 1302.01 of the Revised Code; and "security agreement" shall have the same meaning as defined in section 1309.01 of the Revised Code.

(N) "Finance charge" means the amount which the retail buyer pays or contracts to pay the retail seller for the privilege of paying the principal balance in installments over a period of time. Any advancement in the cash price ordinarily charged by the retail seller is a finance charge when a retail installment sale is made.

(O) "Service charge" means the amount which the retail

buyer pays or contracts to pay the retail seller for the privilege of paying the principal balance in installments over a period of time in addition to the finance charge for the same privilege.

(P) "CONSUMER TRANSACTION" MEANS A SALE, LEASE, ASSIGNMENT, AWARD BY CHANCE, OR OTHER TRANSFER OF AN ITEM OF GOODS, A SERVICE, FRANCHISE, OR AN INTANGIBLE, EXCEPT THOSE TRANSACTIONS BETWEEN PERSONS, DEFINED IN SECTIONS 1905.03 AND 5725.01 OF THE REVISED CODE, AND THEIR CUSTOMERS, OR TRANSACTIONS INVOLVING SALE OR LEASE OF A MOTOR VEHICLE AS DEFINED IN SECTION 4501.01 OF THE REVISED CODE OR MOBILE HOMES, OR BETWEEN ATTORNEYS OR PHYSICIANS AND THEIR CLIENTS OR PATIENTS, TO AN INDIVIDUAL FOR PURPOSES THAT ARE PRIMARILY PERSONAL, FAMILY, OR HOUSEHOLD.

Sec. 1317.031. (A) NOTWITHSTANDING SECTION 1303.34 OF THE REVISED CODE, A RETAIL BUYER WHO EXECUTES AN INSTALLMENT NOTE IN CONNECTION WITH A CONSUMER TRANSACTION MAY ASSERT AS A DEFENSE TO A CLAIM BY A HOLDER IN DUE COURSE AS DEFINED IN SECTION 1303.31 OF THE REVISED CODE, ANY DEFENSE WHICH THE BUYER MAY ASSERT AGAINST THE RETAIL SELLER, UNLESS:

(1) THE HOLDER OR RETAIL SELLER HAS SENT OR DELIVERED TO THE BUYER A NOTICE COMPLYING WITH DIVISION (B) OF THIS SECTION.

(2) THE HOLDER HAS NOT, BEFORE THE DATE SPECIFIED IN SUCH NOTICE, RECEIVED WRITTEN NOTICE THAT THERE EXISTS A CLAIM OR DEFENSE ARISING OUT OF THAT CONSUMER TRANSACTION IN WHICH SUCH NOTE WAS EXECUTED, AND BEEN APPRISED WITH REASONABLE SPECIFICITY OF THE NATURE OF SUCH CLAIM OR DEFENSE. IN THE EXTENT SUCH NOTICE IS RECEIVED BY THE HOLDER HE SHALL NOT BE A HOLDER IN DUE COURSE ONLY AS TO THE CLAIM OR DEFENSE SPECIFIED IN THE NOTICE.

(B) A NOTICE PURSUANT TO DIVISION (A) (1) OF THIS SECTION SHALL:

(1) BE DELIVERED TO THE DEBTOR OR SENT BY

CERTIFIED MAIL TO THE DEBTOR AT HIS LAST KNOWN ADDRESS;

(2) CONTAIN THE NAME AND ADDRESS OF THE HOLDER OF THE NOTE OR OF THE PERSON TO WHOM THE NOTE IS TO BE NEGOTIATED, THE NAME AND ADDRESS OF THE RETAIL SELLER OR OF THE PERSON FROM WHOM THE HOLDER PURCHASED THE NOTE, AND THE AMOUNT DUE UNDER THE NOTE;

(3) CONTAIN A DEADLINE DATE FOR REPLY BY THE BUYER, WHICH SHALL NOT BE EARLIER THAN THE DAY APPLICABLE UNDER DIVISION (C) OF THIS SECTION;

(4) CONTAIN THE FOLLOWING PARAGRAPH, SEPARATE FROM ALL OTHER INFORMATION IN SUCH NOTICE, AND IN SUCH TYPE SIZE OR DISTINCTIVE MARKING THAT IT APPEARS MORE CLEARLY AND CONSPICUOUSLY THAN ANYTHING ELSE IN THE NOTICE:

"WARNING – YOUR NOTE HAS BEEN TRANSFERRED TO ....(THE HOLDER). IF YOU HAVE A CLAIM OR DEFENSE AGAINST THE SELLER OF THE GOODS OR SERVICES FOR WHICH YOU SIGNED THIS NOTE, YOU MUST INFORM ....(THE HOLDER) IN WRITING OF YOUR CLAIM BEFORE ....(DATE) OR YOU WILL BE REQUIRED TO CONTINUE PAYMENTS EVEN THOUGH YOUR CLAIM OR DEFENSE IS VALID."

(C) THE DATE SPECIFIED IN THE WARNING REQUIRED BY DIVISION (B) (4) OF THIS SECTION SHALL NOT BE EARLIER THAN THE FIFTEENTH DAY AFTER:

(1) THE DATE THE GOODS OR SERVICES CONTRACTED FOR ARE FULLY FURNISHED TO THE BUYER, IF THE CONTRACT REQUIRES OR CONTEMPLATES THAT SUCH GOODS OR SERVICES BE FULLY FURNISHED TO THE BUYER WITHIN NINETY DAYS AFTER THE DATE THE INSTRUMENT IS ISSUED;

(2) THE DATE THE FIRST PART OF THE GOODS OR SERVICES CONTRACTED FOR ARE FURNISHED TO THE BUYER, IF THE CONTRACT REQUIRES OR CONTEMPLATES THAT ANY PART OF SUCH GOODS OR SERVICES BE FURNISHED TO THE BUYER MORE THAN NINETY DAYS AFTER

THE DATE THE INSTRUMENT IS ISSUED;

(3) THE DATE SUCH NOTICE IS MAILED OR DELIVERED TO THE BUYER, IF LATER THAN THE DATE SPECIFIED IN DIVISION (C) (1) OR (C) (2) OF THIS SECTION.

(D) TO THE EXTENT THAT A HOLDER IS SUBJECT TO A DEFENSE OF THE BUYER UNDER THIS SECTION, THE HOLDER'S LIABILITY SHALL NOT EXCEED THE AMOUNT OWING TO THE HOLDER ON THE NOTE AT THE TIME THE HOLDER OR RETAIL SELLER GIVES OR DELIVERS NOTICE AS REQUIRED BY DIVISION (A) (1) OF THIS SECTION.

Sec. 1317.06 (A) A retail seller at the time of making any retail installment sale may charge and contract for the payment of a finance charge by the retail buyer and collect and receive the same, which shall not exceed the rates as follows:

(1) A base finance charge at the rate of eight dollars per one hundred dollars per year on the principal balance of the retail installment contract. On retail installment contracts providing for principal balances less than, nor not in multiples of one hundred dollars, or for installment payments extending for a period less than or greater than one year, said finance charge shall be computed proportionately.

(2) In addition to the base finance charge, the retail seller may charge and contract for a service charge of fifty cents per month for the first fifty dollar unit or fraction thereof, of the principal balance for each month of the term of the installment contract; and an additional service charge of twenty-five cents per month for each of the next five fifty dollar units or fraction thereof, of the principal balance for each month of the term of the installment contract.

Such base finance charge and service charges may be computed on a basis of a full month for any fractional period in excess of ten days. For a fractional period of a month not in excess of ten days, there shall be no base finance charge or service charge.

Sections 1317.01 to 1317.11 inclusive of the Revised Code do not apply to any sale in which the base finance and service charge does not exceed the sum of fifteen dollars.

(B) Every retail seller may, at the time of making any retail installment sale, contract for the payment by the retail buyer of lawful delinquent charges as follows:

(1) No charges shall be made for delinquent payments less than ten days late.

(2) Five cents for each dollar for a delinquent payment that is more than ten days late may be charged, but in no event shall a delinquent charge for any one installment exceed three dollars.

A provision for the payment of interest after maturity at a rate not to exceed eight per cent per annum straight interest is not a delinquent charge providing no other charge is made on account of the delinquency.

(C) NO RETAIL INSTALLMENT CONTRACT ARISING OUT OF A CONSUMER TRANSACTION AND REQUIRING THE PAYMENT OF THE CHARGES AUTHORIZED BY THIS SECTION SHALL BE EXECUTED UNLESS THE COMBINED TOTAL OF THE CASH PRICE AND ALL FINANCE CHARGES AND SERVICE CHARGES IS REQUIRED TO BE PAID ACCORDING TO A SCHEDULE OF SUBSTANTIALLY EQUAL CONSECUTIVE INSTALLMENTS, EXCEPT WHERE THE CONTRACT CONTAINS A PROVISION ALLOWING THE BUYER TO REFINANCE THE CONTRACT UNDER TERMS NO LESS FAVORABLE THAN THOSE OF THE ORIGINAL CONTRACT AFTER MAKING THE REFUND CREDIT REQUIRED BY SECTION 1317.09 OF THE REVISED CODE. NO SELLER SHALL, PURSUANT TO ANY PROVISION IN A RETAIL INSTALLMENT CONTRACT ARISING OUT OF A CONSUMER TRANSACTION ACCELERATE ANY PAYMENTS ON ACCOUNT OF A DEFAULT IN THE MAKING OF AN INSTALLMENT PAYMENT THAT HAS NOT CONTINUED FOR AT LEAST THIRTY DAYS. DIVISION (C) OF THIS SECTION DOES NOT APPLY TO THE EXTENT THAT THE PAYMENT SCHEDULE IS ADJUSTED TO THE SEASONAL OR IRREGULAR INCOME OF THE BUYER.

Sec. 1317.07. No retail installment contract authorized by section 1317.03 of the Revised Code which is executed in connection with any retail installment sale shall evidence any indebtedness in excess of the time balance fixed in the written instrument in compliance with section 1317.04 of the Revised Code, but it may evidence in addition any agreements of the parties for the payment of delinquent charges, as provided for in section 1317.06 of the Revised Code, taxes, and any lawful fee actually paid out, or to be paid out, by the retail seller to any public officer for filing, recording, or releasing any instrument securing the payment of the obligation owed on any retail installment contract. No retail seller, directly or indirectly, shall charge, contract for, or receive from any retail buyer, any further or other amount for examination, service, brokerage, commission, expense, fee, or other thing of value. A documentary service charge customarily and presently being paid on May 9, 1949, in a particular business and area shall not be prohibited if the same does not exceed five dollars per sale.

NO RETAIL SELLER SHALL USE MULTIPLE AGREE-MENTS WITH RESPECT TO A SINGLE ITEM OR RELATED ITEMS PURCHASED AT THE SAME TIME, WITH INTENT TO OBTAIN A HIGHER CHARGE THAN WOULD OTHERWISE BE PERMITTED BY CHAPTER 1317. OF THE REVISED CODE OR TO AVOID DISCLOSURE OF AN ANNUAL PERCENTAGE RATE, NOR BY USE OF SUCH AGREEMENTS MAKE ANY CHARGE GREATER THAN THAT WHICH WOULD BE PER-MITTED BY CHAPTER 1317. OF THE REVISED CODE HAD A SINGLE AGREEMENT BEEN USED.

Sec. 1317.071. NO RETAIL SELLER, IN CONNECTION WITH A RETAIL INSTALLMENT CONTRACT ARISING OUT OF A CONSUMER TRANSACTION, SHALL TAKE ANY SECUR-ITY INTEREST OTHER THAN AS AUTHORIZED BY THIS SECTION.

A SELLER MAY TAKE A SECURITY INTEREST IN THE PROPERTY SOLD, AND IN GOODS UPON WHICH SERVICES ARE PERFORMED OR IN WHICH GOODS SOLD ARE IN-STALLED OR TO WHICH THEY ARE ANNEXED.

A SELLER MAY SECURE THE DEBT ARISING FROM THE SALE BY CONTRACTING FOR A SECURITY INTEREST IN OTHER PROPERTY IF, AS A RESULT OF A PRIOR SALE, THE SELLER HAS AN EXISTING SECURITY INTEREST IN THE OTHER PROPERTY, AND HE MAY CONTRACT FOR A SECUR-ITY INTEREST IN THE PROPERTY SOLD IN THE SUBSE-QUENT SALE AS SECURITY FOR THE PREVIOUS DEBT. IF DEBTS ARISING FROM TWO OR MORE SALES ARE THUS SECURED OR ARE CONSOLIDATED INTO ONE DEBT PAY-ABLE ON A SINGLE SCHEDULE OF PAYMENTS, AND THE DEBT IS SECURED BY SECURITY INTERESTS TAKEN WITH

RESPECT TO ONE OR MORE OF THE SALES, PAYMENTS RECEIVED BY THE SELLER AFTER THE TAKING OF SECURITY INTERESTS IN THE OTHER PROPERTY OR THE CONSOLIDATION ARE DEEMED, FOR THE PURPOSE OF DETERMINING THE AMOUNT OF THE DEBT SECURED BY THE VARIOUS SECURITY INTERESTS, TO HAVE BEEN FIRST APPLIED TO THE PAYMENT OF THE DEBTS ARISING FROM THE SALES FIRST MADE. TO THE EXTENT DEBTS ARE PAID ACCORDING TO THIS SECTION, SECURITY INTERESTS IN ITEMS OF PROPERTY TERMINATE AS THE DEBT ORIGINALLY IS PAID.

PAYMENTS RECEIVED BY THE SELLER UPON A REVOLVING CHARGE ACCOUNT ARE DEEMED, FOR THE PURPOSE OF DETERMINING THE AMOUNT OF THE DEBT SECURED BY THE VARIOUS SECURITY INTERESTS, TO HAVE BEEN APPLIED FIRST TO THE PAYMENT OF CREDIT SERVICE CHARGES IN THE ORDER OF THEIR ENTRY TO THE ACCOUNT AND THEN TO THE PAYMENT OF DEBTS IN THE ORDER IN WHICH THE ENTRIES TO THE ACCOUNT SHOWING THE DEBTS WERE MADE.

IF THE DEBTS CONSOLIDATED AROSE FROM TWO OR MORE SALES MADE ON THE SAME DAY, PAYMENTS RECEIVED BY THE SELLER ARE DEEMED, FOR THE PURPOSE OF DETERMINING THE AMOUNT OF THE DEBT SECURED BY THE VARIOUS SECURITY INTERESTS, TO HAVE BEEN APPLIED FIRST TO THE PAYMENT OF THE SMALLEST DEBT.

Sec. 1317.12. NOTWITHSTANDING ANY AGREEMENT TO THE CONTRARY IN A RETAIL INSTALLMENT CONTRACT MADE ON OR AFTER THE EFFECTIVE DATE OF THIS SECTION, IF COLLATERAL FOR A CONSUMER TRANSACTION IS TAKEN POSSESSION OF BY THE SECURED PARTY ON DEFAULT, THE SECURED PARTY SHALL, WITHIN FIVE BUSINESS DAYS AFTER TAKING POSSESSION, SEND TO THE DEBTOR A NOTICE SETTING FORTH SPECIFICALLY THE CIRCUMSTANCES CONSTITUTING THE DEFAULT AND THE AMOUNT BY ITEMIZATION THAT THE DEBTOR IS REQUIRED TO PAY TO CURE HIS DEFAULT. ANY NOTICE REQUIRED BY SECTION 1309.47 or 1317.16 OF THE REVISED CODE MAY BE INCLUDED AS PART OF THE NOTICE REQUIRED BY THIS SECTION. A SECURED PARTY WHO DISPOSES OF THE COLLATERAL WITHOUT SENDING NOTICE REQUIRED BY THIS SECTION MAY NOT RECOVER THE

COSTS OF RETAKING POSSESSION OF THE COLLATERAL AND IS NOT ENTITLED TO A DEFICIENCY JUDGMENT.

THE DEBTOR MAY CURE HIS DEFAULT WITHIN TWENTY DAYS AFTER THE SECURED PARTY RETAKES POSSESSION OF THE COLLATERAL, OR WITHIN FIFTEEN DAYS AFTER THE SECURED PARTY SENDS THE NOTICE REQUIRED BY THIS SECTION, WHICHEVER IS LATER, BY DELIVERING TO THE SECURED PARTY THE FOLLOWING:

(A) ALL INSTALLMENTS DUE OR PAST DUE AT THE TIME OF SUCH DELIVERY;

(B) ANY UNPAID DELINQUENCY OR DEFERRED CHARGES;

(C) THE ACTUAL AND REASONABLE EXPENSES INCURRED BY THE SECURED PARTY IN RETAKING POSSESSION OF THE COLLATERAL PROVIDED THAT ANY PORTION OF SUCH EXPENSES WHICH EXCEEDS TWENTY-FIVE DOLLARS NEED NOT BE DELIVERED TO THE SECURED PARTY PURSUANT TO THIS DIVISION, BUT SHALL BE ADDED TO THE TIME BALANCE;

(D) A DEPOSIT BY CASH OR BOND IN THE AMOUNT OF TWO INSTALLMENTS, TO SECURE THE TIMELY PAYMENT OF FUTURE INSTALLMENTS BY THE DEBTOR. THE SECURED PARTY MAY APPLY SUCH CASH OR THE PROCEEDS OF SUCH BOND TOWARD THE SATISFACTION OF THE DEBT IN THE EVENT OF ANOTHER DEFAULT BY THE DEBTOR.

DURING THE PERIOD BETWEEN THE TIME A SECURED PARTY RETAKES POSSESSION OF THE COLLATERAL AND THE EXPIRATION OR EXERCISE OF THE DEBTOR'S RIGHT TO CURE HIS DEFAULT, THE SECURED PARTY SHALL MAKE THE COLLATERAL AVAILABLE FOR INSPECTION BY THE DEBTOR DURING REASONABLE HOURS.

IF THE DEBTOR CURES HIS DEFAULT, HE MAY TAKE POSSESSION OF THE COLLATERAL. THE SECURED PARTY SHALL ASSEMBLE THE COLLATERAL AND MAKE IT AVAILABLE TO THE DEBTOR AT A TIME AND PLACE THAT IS REASONABLY CONVENIENT TO BOTH PARTIES. IF THE DEBTOR REQUESTS THE SECURED PARTY TO RETURN THE COLLATERAL TO THE PLACE FROM WHICH IT WAS TAKEN, THE SECURED PARTY MAY CHARGE THE DEBTOR THE ACTUAL AND REASONABLE EXPENSES INCURRED IN RETURNING THE COLLATERAL TO THE PLACE FROM WHICH

IT WAS TAKEN, WHICH AMOUNT SHALL BE ADDED TO THE TIME BALANCE.

A DEBTOR'S RIGHT TO CURE HIS DEFAULT PURSUANT TO THIS SECTION MAY NOT BE EXERCISED MORE THAN ONCE WITH RESPECT TO A SINGLE DEBT.

A SECURED PARTY WHO REASONABLY BELIEVES THAT A DEBTOR INTENDS TO CONCEAL OR REMOVE THE COLLATERAL FROM THIS STATE AFTER CURING HIS DEFAULT MAY, WITHIN FIVE DAYS AFTER RETAKING POSSESSION OF THE COLLATERAL, MOVE IN A COURT OF COMPETENT JURISDICTION THAT HE BE ALLOWED TO RETAIN POSSESSION OF THE COLLATERAL AS SECURITY FOR THE DEBT. IF THE COURT FINDS REASONABLE CAUSE TO BELIEVE THAT THE DEBTOR INTENDS TO CONCEAL THE COLLATERAL OR REMOVE IT FROM THIS STATE, IT SHALL ORDER THAT THE COLLATERAL REMAIN IN THE POSSESSION OF THE SECURED PARTY, NOTWITHSTANDING THE OTHER PROVISIONS OF THIS SECTION. IF THE DEBTOR CURES HIS DEFAULT, THE SECURED PARTY SHALL NOT DISPOSE OF THE COLLATERAL UNLESS THE DEBTOR AGAIN DEFAULTS, AND HE SHALL MAKE SUCH COLLATERAL AVAILABLE TO THE DEBTOR WHEN THE DEBT IS PAID IN FULL.

Sec. 1317.13 NOTWITHSTANDING THE PROVISIONS OF SECTION 1309.46 OF THE REVISED CODE OR ANY AGREEMENT BY THE PARTIES TO A CONSUMER TRANSACTION TO THE CONTRARY, A SECURED PARTY WHOSE SECURITY INTEREST IS TAKEN PURSUANT TO SECTION 1317.071 OF THE REVISED CODE, SHALL NOT BE ENTITLED TO TAKE POSSESSION OF THE COLLATERAL UPON DEFAULT BY THE DEBTOR IF THE TIME BALANCE AT THE TIME OF THE DEFAULT IS LESS THAN TWENTY-FIVE PERCENT OF THE SUM OF THE TIME BALANCE ON THE DAY SUCH RETAIL INSTALLMENT CONTRACT WAS EXECUTED AND THE DOWN PAYMENT RECITED IN SUCH CONTRACT.

Sec. 1317.14. (A) WHEN CONTAINED IN A RETAIL INSTALLMENT CONTRACT ARISING OUT OF A CONSUMER TRANSACTION, AN AGREEMENT BY THE BUYER OR LESSEE NOT TO ASSERT AGAINST AN ASSIGNEE A CLAIM OR DEFENSE ARISING OUT OF THE SALE OR LEASE IS ENFORCEABLE ONLY BY AN ASSIGNEE WHO ACQUIRES THE BUYER'S OR LESSEE'S CONTRACT IN GOOD FAITH AND

FOR VALUE, AND WHOSE ASSIGNOR GIVES THE BUYER OR LESSEE NOTICE OF THE ASSIGNMENT AS PROVIDED IN THIS SECTION AND WHO, WITHIN THE TIME PERIOD APPLICABLE UNDER DIVISION (D) OF THIS SECTION, RECEIVES NO WRITTEN NOTICE OF THE FACTS GIVING RISE TO THE BUYER'S OR LESSEE'S DEFENSE. SUCH AGREEMENT NOT TO ASSERT A CLAIM OR DEFENSE IS ENFORCEABLE ONLY WITH RESPECT TO DEFENSES WHICH HAVE ARISEN AFTER THE END OF THE APPLICABLE PERIOD OR WHICH AROSE DURING SUCH PERIOD BUT OF WHICH THE BUYER OR LESSEE GAVE THE ASSIGNEE NO NOTICE AS PROVIDED IN THIS SECTION. THE NOTICE OF ASSIGNMENT SHALL BE IN WRITING AND ADDRESSED TO THE BUYER OR LESSEE AT HIS ADDRESS AS STATED IN THE CONTRACT, IDENTIFY THE CONTRACT, DESCRIBE THE GOODS OR SERVICES, AND STATE THE NAMES OF THE SELLER OR LESSOR AND BUYER OR LESSEE, THE NAME AND ADDRESS OF THE ASSIGNEE OR THE PERSON TO WHOM THE CONTRACT IS TO BE ASSIGNED, THE AMOUNT PAYABLE BY THE BUYER OR LESSEE AND THE NUMBER, AMOUNTS, AND DUE DATES OF THE INSTALLMENTS. IN ADDITION, SUCH NOTICE SHALL CONTAIN A CONSPICUOUS WARNING TO THE BUYER OR LESSEE THAT HE HAS A CERTAIN PERIOD WITHIN WHICH TO NOTIFY THE ASSIGNEE IN WRITING OF ANY COMPLAINTS OR DEFENSES HE MAY HAVE AGAINST THE SELLER OR LESSOR, THAT SUCH PERIOD EXPIRES ON A DATE, TO BE SPECIFIED IN SUCH WARNING, WHICH SHALL NOT BE EARLIER THAN THE LAST DAY OF THE PERIOD APPLICABLE UNDER DIVISION (D) OF THIS SECTION, AND THAT IF WRITTEN NOTIFICATION OF THE DEFENSES IS NOT RECEIVED BY THE ASSIGNEE WITHIN THE APPLICABLE PERIOD, THE ASSIGNEE WILL HAVE THE RIGHT TO ENFORCE THE CONTRACT FREE OF ANY DEFENSES THE BUYER OR LESSEE MAY HAVE AGAINST THE SELLER OR LESSOR.

(B) AN ASSIGNEE DOES NOT ACQUIRE A BUYER'S OR LESSEE'S CONTRACT IN GOOD FAITH WITHIN THE MEANING OF DIVISION (A) OF THIS SECTION IF THE ASSIGNEE HAS KNOWLEDGE OR, FROM HIS COURSE OF DEALING WITH THE SELLER OR LESSOR OR HIS RECORDS, NOTICE OF SUBSTANTIAL COMPLAINTS BY OTHER BUYERS OR LESSEES OF THE SELLER'S OR LESSOR'S FAILURE OR

REFUSAL TO PERFORM HIS CONTRACTS WITH THEM AND OF THE SELLER'S OR LESSOR'S FAILURE TO REMEDY HIS DEFAULTS WITHIN A REASONABLE TIME AFTER THE ASSIGNEE NOTIFIES HIM OF THE COMPLAINTS.

(C) TO THE EXTENT THAT UNDER THIS SECTION AN ASSIGNEE IS SUBJECT TO DEFENSES OF THE BUYER OR LESSEE AGAINST THE SELLER OR LESSOR, RIGHTS OF THE BUYER OR LESSEE UNDER THIS SECTION CAN ONLY BE ASSERTED AS A MATTER OF DEFENSE TO A CLAIM BY THE ASSIGNEE, AND THE ASSIGNEE'S LIABILITY UNDER THIS SECTION SHALL NOT EXCEED THE AMOUNT OWING TO THE ASSIGNEE ON THE CONTRACT AT THE TIME THE ASSIGNOR GIVES NOTICE AS REQUIRED BY DIVISION (A) OF THIS SECTION.

(D) NOTWITHSTANDING ANY AGREEMENT TO THE CONTRARY, THE PERIOD DURING WHICH A BUYER OR LESSEE MAY NOTIFY AN ASSIGNEE OF A CLAIM OR DEFENSE ARISING OUT OF THE SALE OR LEASE SHALL TERMINATE ON THE FIFTEENTH DAY AFTER:
(1) THE DATE THE GOODS OR SERVICES CONTRACTED FOR ARE FULLY FURNISHED TO THE BUYER, IF THE CONTRACT REQUIRES OR CONTEMPLATES THAT SUCH GOODS OR SERVICES BE FULLY FURNISHED TO THE BUYER WITHIN NINETY DAYS AFTER THE DATE THE CONTRACT IS EXECUTED;
(2) THE DATE THE FIRST PART OF THE GOODS OR SERVICES CONTRACTED FOR ARE FURNISHED TO THE BUYER, IF THE CONTRACT REQUIRES OR CONTEMPLATES THAT ANY PART OF SUCH GOODS OR SERVICES BE FURNISHED TO THE BUYER MORE THAN NINETY DAYS AFTER THE DATE THE CONTRACT IS EXECUTED;
(3) THE DATE SUCH NOTICE IS MAILED OR DELIVERED TO THE BUYER, IF LATER THAN THE DATE SPECIFIED IN DIVISION (D) (1) OR (D) (2) OF THIS SECTION.

Sec. 1317.16. (A) A SECURED PARTY WHOSE SECURITY INTEREST IS TAKEN PURSUANT TO SECTION 1317.071 OF THE REVISED CODE MAY, AFTER DEFAULT, DISPOSE OF ANY OR ALL OF THE COLLATERAL ONLY AS AUTHORIZED BY THIS SECTION.

(B) DISPOSITION OF THE COLLATERAL SHALL BE

BY PUBLIC SALE ONLY. SUCH SALE MAY BE AS A UNIT OR IN PARCELS AND THE METHOD, MANNER, TIME, PLACE, AND TERMS THEREOF SHALL BE COMMERCIALLY REASONABLE. AT LEAST TEN DAYS PRIOR TO SALE THE SECURED PARTY SHALL SEND NOTIFICATION OF THE TIME AND PLACE OF SUCH SALE AND OF THE MINIMUM PRICE FOR WHICH SUCH COLLATERAL WILL BE SOLD, TOGETHER WITH A STATEMENT THAT THE DEBTOR MAY BE HELD LIABLE FOR ANY DEFICIENCY RESULTING FROM SUCH SALE, BY CERTIFIED MAIL, RETURN RECEIPT REQUESTED, TO THE DEBTOR AT HIS LAST ADDRESS KNOWN TO THE SECURED PARTY, AND TO ANY PERSONS KNOWN BY THE SECURED PARTY TO HAVE AN INTEREST IN THE COLLATERAL. IN ADDITION, THE SECURED PARTY SHALL CAUSE TO BE PUBLISHED, AT LEAST TEN DAYS PRIOR TO THE SALE, A NOTICE OF SUCH SALE LISTING THE ITEMS TO BE SOLD, IN A NEWSPAPER OF GENERAL CIRCULATION IN THE COUNTY WHERE THE SALE IS TO BE HELD.

(C) EXCEPT AS MODIFIED BY THIS SECTION, SECTION 1309.47 OF THE REVISED CODE GOVERNS DISPOSITION OF COLLATERAL BY THE SECURED PARTY.

INDEX